POETRY OF THE BODY

POETRY OF THE BODY

Stories about Acupuncture Points

DEANNA SLATE STENNETT, L.AC., MA

iUniverse

POETRY OF THE BODY
STORIES ABOUT ACUPUNCTURE POINTS

Copyright © 2018 Deanna Slate Stennett, L.Ac., MA.

All rights reserved. No part of this book may be used or reproduced by any means, graphic, electronic, or mechanical, including photocopying, recording, taping or by any information storage retrieval system without the written permission of the author except in the case of brief quotations embodied in critical articles and reviews.

iUniverse books may be ordered through booksellers or by contacting:

iUniverse
1663 Liberty Drive
Bloomington, IN 47403
www.iuniverse.com
1-800-Authors (1-800-288-4677)

Because of the dynamic nature of the Internet, any web addresses or links contained in this book may have changed since publication and may no longer be valid. The views expressed in this work are solely those of the author and do not necessarily reflect the views of the publisher, and the publisher hereby disclaims any responsibility for them.

Any people depicted in stock imagery provided by Getty Images are models, and such images are being used for illustrative purposes only. Certain stock imagery © Getty Images.

ISBN: 978-1-5320-5706-9 (sc)
ISBN: 978-1-5320-5705-2 (e)

Library of Congress Control Number: 2018910399

Print information available on the last page.

iUniverse rev. date: 09/10/2018

Foreword
by Tom Balles, L.Ac., M.Ac.

The healing modalities of acupuncture and shamanism are thousands of years old. It would be impossible for either of them to *not* be rooted in nature - in an Earth that is alive and filled with spirits. In this pioneering work Deanna Stennett becomes the first to reveal how these two modalities can be woven into a single, beautiful fabric. Through the use of shamanic journeys we come to meet the spirits of the acupuncture points.

The first sections of the book walk us through the seasons, of which there are five in this framework (1. Autumn, 2. Winter, 3. Spring, 4. Summer, and 5. Late Summer). Our eyes are opened to the many gifts, capacities, and qualities that accompany each season. Since we are a part of nature, we then get to explore how those same gifts, capacities, and qualities reside in us.

A particular emotion - grief, fear, anger, joy, and sympathy – also corresponds to each season. Deanna expands our traditional ways of understanding these emotions so we can experience each of them as multi-faceted, transformative, and life-affirming.

Stories follow in each section. At times Deanna shares some of her personal story as well as those of classmates, friends, and patients. These accounts of challenges, obstacles, and the pains of life are all too familiar.

Then come the journeys to the spirit of acupuncture points. We can almost hear the rhythmic beating of the drum, sink into our own bodies at the location of the acupuncture point, and continue falling and falling into new landscapes.

The shamanic terrains are lands of sensual delights, the details striking. The experiences are as rich, juicy, and alive as if one were walking in the woods. You can feel the cool breezes and the moist grass underneath your feet, touch the trees, and smell the flowers. The journeys connect our senses with Nature both inside and outside ourselves.

While exploring the landscape the spirits come to visit. Each is a unique and compelling character. For example, the spirit of Side Passage (Large Intestine 6) is a "peculiar little man about five feet tall, with curly red hair who is graying at the temples. He wears a plaid shirt and khaki beige shorts that come to just below his knees . . .he has little round spectacles on the tip of his nose, round rosy cheeks, and a slight grin."Sometimes warm and welcoming, sometimes daunting, each spirit has powerful medicine to share.

Upon meeting a spirit, Deanna states her desire as a practitioner: "I want to know the medicine of this place and how to use it for my patients." What a humble and respectful plea, one that could be made of any of our teachers, no matter the healing modality.

The spirits respond with humor, wit, and wisdom. They share new ways as to when, where, and how the gifts of that acupuncture point can be offered to a patient. We come to know each point in very different ways.

In one example, the acupuncture point Gate of Hope (Liver 14), offers her wise counsel, "Use this point to help your patients know that whatever they are experiencing as painful, dark, or hopeless will end. The Sun will rise. The Spring will come. Life will start again, over and over again. This is what hope is all about. Having hope doesn't mean you will never experience difficult or challenging times; it means that it won't last."

The spirits act as powerful reminders of the wisdom and resources that already reside within each of us. How different my acupuncture career would have been had I known at the beginning how to take these journeys. I would have understood more deeply what is meant by the "spirit of the point" as used in acupuncture.

As a practitioner I've watched for over thirty years as acupuncture has "melted" into the great melting pot that is America. Our ways of "knowing" in the West tend toward the physical, mechanical, and scientific. Esteemed colleagues have been eager to study, research, and then standardize components like point locations, needle techniques, and acupuncture treatments.

In *Poetry of the Body*, Deanna reminds us of another path, another way of "knowing". She invites us to an embodied practice that is neither generic nor prescriptive. Shamanic journeys are of the particular: performed by a particular practitioner, using a particular point, for a particular patient, in order to contact a particular spirit. She succeeds in adding a new layer and another dimension to how we can understand spirit in Chinese medicine.

Deanna is an experienced frequent traveler beyond the veil. I encourage you to join her in journeying to that land. You'll find Deanna to be a most engaging guide along the way. Don't forget that most respectful and humble plea to be made of the spirits, "Please tell me about your medicine and how to use it for my patients". Precious indeed will be the rewards.

Tom Balles, L.Ac., M.Ac.
Author of *Dancing with the Ten Thousand Things* and *Becoming a Healing Presence.*

December, 2017

Acknowledgements

This book has been a work in progress for a long time. I first want to thank Great Spirit who inspired me, nagged me, and lovingly gave me the images and visions for this project. I want to thank and acknowledge my parents who always told me that I should be a writer. I want to thank my daughters who have given me some of the stories included in this book and expressed their pride in me for writing it. I want to thank my partner, Missy Carney who has encouraged and supported me through this process. My editor, Elise Hancock - thank you for the hours we spent together in your home, sipping tea, typing, sharing stories and clarifying. Without you this book would not have the cohesion and crispness it has. I also want to thank Karen Devonshire for the second editing, and for being a long time dear friend. I want to thank my teacher, Sandra Ingerman, for all her encouragement. Sandy, your approachability and humility combined with your lifetime of serving spirit and helping others, and your great knowledge has been a source of inspiration and determination. Another teacher who has helped me see the lineage of shamanism in my own ancestry is Tom Cowan. Thank you for your Celtic Shamanism training. I want to thank my acupuncturist, Tom Balles, for his support and encouragement, as well as his gift of writing the Foreword for me. A huge thank you to my friends, patients, and students, (of both Acupuncture and Shamanism), for expressing your interest and desire for me to write this book so you could read and learn from it. Finally, to all of you who donated to the Gofundme so I could publish this book, a big hug of gratitude!

Introduction

I am a daydreamer: I often space out and find stories running through my head, and I also have very vivid sleeping dreams. I don't often have spontaneous visions, though when they come, I pay attention. I was 45 when this vision of my old age came to me. It was clear, I felt as if I were right there. I didn't even realize the experience was a vision till it was over.

"Are you asleep, Gran?"

She startled me out of my conversation with the spirits. Most of my life I have had a running conversation with the spirits, and now that my eyesight is almost gone, I "see" them more vividly. The distractions of everyday reality no longer get in the way.

My great-granddaughter is reading in the room with me, and when she speaks I look in her direction. She is sitting on the floor by the fireplace, and I can hear the fire crackling. I have a blanket across my lap, and I am rocking in the rocking chair. There are colors flowing out in every breath she exhales, and from her eyes. I always knew the colors existed, but only in old age do I experience them so vividly.

"Yes, sweetheart?"

"Tell me again what he calls you. You know, that plant you talk with. What does he call you?"

I smile as I recall my first encounter with Mugwort in the spirit realm. He was a willowy, leafy spirit, and he told me that when I speak with him, I should always identify myself as "the healer who sees beauty in all things." I relay that to her and she goes back to her book. I feel grateful that she is growing up with the encouragement and teaching that I lacked as a child. However, I was aware of the colors and energy flows at a very early age, because I used to call everyone pretty or beautiful. As a child I was often told that people I thought were beautiful were actually ugly, so I grew up burdened by that contradiction. It took me many years to trust my own sense of the world.

The vision passed and I opened my eyes....

This book is neither a textbook nor a how-to book for acupuncturists. It is a book that explores the relationship of acupuncture points with the living beings who live where the points reside. We all have these points - we were born with them, and the ancient Chinese gave them names. These names aren't anatomy labels such as xiphoid process or femoral artery. They speak to the poetry of the body with names like Abundant Splendor, Spirit Burial Ground and Palace of Weariness. There are many books in this century that speak eloquently about the spirits of the points and their names, based on translations of their Chinese characters. I did not write another one of those books.

It is also commonly agreed that each point "has a spirit." One interpretation is that the word spirit means the essence or quality of the point, while another interpretation holds that there are actual spirit beings who are the points. I believe both are true, and having a background in Shamanic Studies chose to meet the spirit beings who *are* the points. In this book we will meet some of them.

When I was in Acupuncture school, a shaman came to our school as a guest lecturer. This was my introduction to shamanism and shamanic journeying. After graduating, I began to search for more training in shamanism. I found The Foundation for Shamanic Studies (FSS), whose main headquarters is in Mill Valley, California. They have trained teachers all around the country who run workshops. I had also read Sandra Ingerman's book **Soul Retrieval**, and really wanted to study with her, so I flew to Tucson, Arizona to take my first workshop, even though there were plenty of offerings on the east coast. From there, I took her five-day workshop on Soul Retrieval. I started FSS' 3 year advanced training in 1998. This was taught by Michael Harner and we met at Omega Institute in Upstate New York. Michael suffered a stroke during our second meeting and stopped teaching on the east coast. My beloved teacher, Sandra Ingerman, took over this program. After I graduated from this program, I did a 2 year program in Celtic Shamanism with Tom Cowan, author of **Shamanism as a Spiritual Practice for Daily Life.** I also went on a 10 day tour of Ireland with Tom Cowan, where we journeyed in sacred sites and stone circles. In 2002, I started a 2 year program with Sandra Ingerman for Teacher Training. After graduation, all the teachers from all her programs meet every couple years for continued learning and sharing.

———————————————-o———————————————

In Shamanic practices everything is Spirit. So there is spirit associated with trees, rocks, chairs, body parts: everything. Each spirit is part of the one Spirit, and at the same time has its own characteristics. In Shamanic practices it is common to communicate with the spiritual aspect of something, which is often done by entering an altered (trance-like) state of consciousness to understand its wisdom. The most common way that a Shaman reaches the appropriate state is by listening to rhythms from drum beats, rattles, click sticks, didgeridoo, or Tibetan bowls. These rhythms, when in the range of 120-140 beats per minute have been shown to affect the listener's brain waves taking the person into a theta state - an altered state of consciousness. This altered state of consciousness is commonly referred to as a *Shamanic Journey.*

When someone takes a shamanic journey, various types of sensory experiences can occur. Some people have visions, some hear things, some smell things, some taste or touch things and some receive a "knowing," via a telepathic type of connection. A journey can include any or all of these things. In every case, however, the intention or question is set ahead of time. As soon as the person enters the journey state, whatever the experience, all of it is part of an answer to the question or intention.

I decided to use this method to journey to the spirits of the acupuncture points, not to gather information about the points, but rather to make a connection and establish a relationship with the points. I would hold the intention of meeting the spirit of a particular point, then I would drum (or use a CD) to shift my brain waves. I would then see a large hill in the shape of my own body, and I would go to the point's position on that hill and sink into the point. From then on, the imagery and sensory experience was as unique as each individual point. Always my question for each spirit of the points was the same: "Tell me about your medicine." The word, *medicine,* in native or indigenous cultures is interchangeable with the word, *wisdom.* I was asking the spirits to teach me about their essence, their stories, and their unique manifestations of the one Spirit. As I began doing this, I started to see that the stories of my life and the lives of my friends and patients had wisdom similar to some of the points I met.

In this book I refer to my "animal guide" when I am describing the journeys to the points. Traditional shamans believe that everyone gets an animal spirit, (sometimes referred to as a power animal or totem animal,) at the time of birth. The way it was told to me is that when each child is born an animal spirit looks down on the frail human and has pity on him/her, and says, "I'll watch over this one." Notice that I never tell what my totem animal is. The traditional belief is that naming the animal diminishes its power.

Another thing I did was conduct workshops in which all the students would journey to the same acupuncture point. As it turned out, the journeys would be quite different - *and* there was always a theme or group of images that showed up in all of the journeys. I came to understand clearly there is a universal spirit of the point - the commonality -*and* an individual spirit of the point.

The people who were involved in my workshops were students from Maryland University of Integrative Health (MUIH), (formerly Tai Sophia Institute). I have been teaching in the Acupuncture program since 1999. My students were eager to learn different ways to approach the acupuncture points. I also earned my Master's degree in Transformative Leadership and Social Change at MUIH, and this book was my thesis project, which MUIH calls, "Project of Excellence."

There are some terms that the reader may not be familiar with, such as *Qi.* Qi (pronounced chee) is the substance that flows through all the channels where the points reside. Channels are sometimes called meridians. Qi is electrical/magnetic energy (just like light) and Chinese medicine describes it in many forms. There is Qi that flows in the channels like a circulatory system, touching each of the organs and connecting with each other. There is Qi that is on the surface of the body, which is our protection from external causes of disease, there is Qi which is created by the mixing of breath and food to nourish us. A simple translation is energy. And it is bigger than that. Channels/Meridians are mostly named after the organ where they originate, such as the "Lung Channel".

In *Poetry of the Body,* each chapter starts with a story, either from my life or about my friends or patients. All original names and personal specifics have been changed to protect the privacy of those involved. The story is followed by my journey to the particular point that I feel expresses the essence of the story.

Another thing to keep in mind is that these visions of the points are <u>mine,</u> and as such they often have an aspect that is particular to me. I hope you will also touch the universal spirt of the point, but even so, keep in mind that my book is not a "bible" or "encyclopedia" of acupuncture points. Visions are not set in stone. It is a book exploring possible ways to look at something. There are many, many possibilities and this one that came to me is simply one of those possibilities.

It is my hope that the reader finds wonder and delight in these names and stories, and that they will go on to explore their own relationship with the magic in their own body. I hope it inspires to want to know more about acupuncture points, about stories/spirits that live all around you, about shamanism, about nature . . . and mostly about yourself, for it is in knowing the particular magic that lives in you that you are truly able to serve the world.

Table of Contents

Foreword 1
Acknowledgements 5
Introduction 7

Section 1: Autumn 17
Ch. 1   Joining of the Valleys (Large Intestine 4) 21
Ch. 2   Lawrence and Very Great Abyss (Lung 9) 27
Ch. 3   Leslie and Arnie - Side Passage: (Large Intestines 6) 36

Section 2: Winter 44
Ch. 4   Fear of Death: Dark Gate (Kidney 21) 47
Ch. 5   Peace in Chaos: Fly and Scatter (Bladder 58) 57
Ch. 6   White Feather: Walking on the Verandah (Kidney 22) 66

Section 3: Spring 76
Ch. 7   No Regrets - Gate of Hope (Liver 14) 79
Ch. 8   The Big Picture: Sun and Moon (Gall Bladder 24) 88
Ch. 9   Pets - Foot above Tears (Gall Bladder 42) 96

Section 4: Summer 102
Ch. 10 The Lesson of a Living/Dying Patient: Palace of
         Weariness (Pericardium 8) 107
Ch. 11 My Dad - Nourishing the Old (Small Intestine 6) 114
Ch. 12 Linda and Harriet - Spirit Gate (Heart 7) 122
Ch. 13 Changes - Spirit Path (Heart 5) 128
Ch. 14 Sheri - Assembly of Ancestors (Three Heater 6) 137

Section 5: Late Summer 143
Ch. 15 Did you say Faeries?: Abundant
         Splendor - (Stomach 40) 146
Ch. 16 Gloria and Lillian - Three Yin Crossing: (Spleen 6) 152
Ch. 17 Miracles and Grandmothers - Supreme
         White: (Spleen 3) 157
Ch. 18 Cindy and Earth Granary - (Stomach 4) 166

Section 6: Oceans 171
Ch. 19 Jamie and Dove Tail - (Conception Vessel 15) 173
Ch. 20 Initiation to Spirit - Wind Palace - (Governor Vessel 16) 179

Section 7: Autumn - Again 184
Ch. 21 Welcome Fragrance: (Large Intestines 20) 186
Ch. 22 The Gifts - Fish Region: (Lung 10) 194
Ch. 23 Wrapping it up 201

About The Author 204

Section 1: Autumn

If I had to pick a season I love the most, it would be Autumn, which arrives after the heat and humidity of late Summer have gone on and on until I just can't stand another minute... then those first cool breezes of Autumn come like whispers from heaven. I will literally stand outside with my arms spread, giving thanks to the weather gods. The day I get to wear a sweater and my cheeks turn pink in the early morning coolness, I dance for joy. My steps speed up and I breathe more deeply.

In North America, Autumn is when the leaves turn brilliant colors, then fall. The colors range from bright yellow to fluorescent orange and on to a deep blood red. People actually travel to areas famous for vivid Autumns to enjoy the "peak" of the season. For me, that "peak" is over all too soon.

I believe that all aspects of our planet, and most likely of the entire Universe, are linked in such a way that what happens in the autumnal trees simultaneously happens in other forms of life. In the trees, though, the process is easy to see: to make ready for the chill of Winter, the trees choose what is valuable and worth storing, versus what must be let go. They pull their vital essence to the safety of the roots, depriving the leaves of that essence. So those beautiful colors are actually signs that the leaves are dying. Eventually they fall and turn brown, withered corpses of the beauty they once were.

Mammals, too, spend autumn gathering nourishment to store for the hard times coming. Bears gorge enough food to let them sleep through the winter, while squirrels and other rodents hide their booty where they can find it later. In nature, Autumn is when all forms of life store their valuables where they are safe, yet available, and let go of everything else.

When we humans live in harmony with this season, we too look at our lives and decide what is valuable, that we should hold onto, and what should be let go. The process can apply to our physical belongings, emotional baggage, or spiritual practices. The questions in every case are the same: What is most valuable? What is precious and serves life? What is unnecessary and no longer serves life? The next time we experience Autumn, let's pay attention to life around us, let this season teach us the value of each moment, and of every person, place, or thing that brings joy to us, versus what weighs us down and causes us to suffer.

According to Chinese medicine, the two organs (or "officials," as in officials of the Chinese court) of the Autumn are the Lungs and the Colon. Lungs pull in air, essential to life, while the Colon lets go of what no longer serves. The points we will meet in this chapter are on the two meridians (or energy pathways) associated with these "officials.'

Chinese tradition holds that the emotion of this season is what we call "grief." However, this word is merely a translation of a translation from the ancient Chinese. What modern people mean by "grief" is only the tip of the iceberg of what the ancients meant. To enlarge your sense of the word, think of a moment in your life that was so precious that even as it ended, you were acutely aware of the loss. Would we call that feeling grief? Or might we call it love? I know a man, a fellow acupuncturist, who says that he can't bear to look at pictures of his son as a baby, because it is so painful to realize those moments are already gone. His experience speaks of a love so deep it actually causes him pain to remember individual moments, because in remembering, he knows he can never have those moments again. This "grief" has no consolation. There is nothing anyone can to say make it okay that these precious moments are gone. The only choice is to let them go - at the same time knowing that other moments as precious will come, if we stay open to let them in.

In our Autumns, then, let's be deliberate in deciding what we want to let go. Honor each item - then let it go. Let it be like the brown leaves that fall to the ground and return minerals to the soil as they decompose, for there's a paradox here: in a real sense, the future value of the whatever-it-is depends on letting it go. In the mind and spirit, letting go leaves an empty place for something new. Externally, a released object can then go on to serve again. I have a friend who always says to herself, as she takes treasures to the thrift store, "Someone will be <u>so happy</u> to find this!" Only knowing that allows her to let old treasures go.

Chapter 1: Joining of the Valleys (Large Intestine 4)

My sensitivity to spirit and the healing path, started at a very young age, but I didn't pursue it till I was in my early thirties. Now I look down at the back of my hand to the soft hollow created where the bones of my thumb and forefinger meet. That's where I experienced my very first acupuncture needle as it penetrated my skin and then my soul . . .

It was a smoggy October day in Southern California. The day before had been sparkling clear, a day when the Santa Ana winds blew the smog out to sea. Today, though, the wind was back to normal and the mountains surrounding L.A. were lost again in smog. Such an opening happens two or three times a year, the winds shift and the mountains - which I used to almost forget were there - would appear, as if from a dream. It made me breathless as I drove the freeway, to see the snowcaps so clear and shining against the blue.

My soul at the time was like the mountains - I see that now. It was hidden by a dead marriage and obligated to an oppressive religion that told me that since I was a woman I couldn't use my mind. So I had learned to bury the gifts I was born with until, every once in a while, something would shift, like the Santa Ana winds, and my soul would surface. Then I would bury myself again with the busy-ness of motherhood and nursing a man with a debilitating illness.

I pulled up at the Acupuncture office. The day before I had brought my husband here in a desperate attempt to halt the downward spiral of Multiple Sclerosis. I had sat in the dimly lit office for close to three hours while this man asked hundreds of questions about things not even related to MS. I was envious of the gentle care given to my husband. I'd never seen a healthcare practitioner devote so much focused interest on a patient, and I wanted someone to care about me like that. So here I was. It was *my* turn.

It had been years since I'd wept — five, at least. When my husband and I fought, early in our marriage, I learned not to cry, so I could stand my ground. I buried my feelings with my soul. After I answered the acupuncturist's questions, he placed the needles — the first one going into that hollow on my hand.

Each of the points, I was to learn later, had names and spirits. This point is called "Joining of the Valleys," or sometimes "The Great Eliminator." I felt an urge to cry as the needle touched my skin, I was fighting tears as I left the office, and I couldn't contain them as I drove home. The mountains were out to stay.

Joining of the Valleys - The Journey

Alone in my living room, I put the CD into the stereo and pushed play. As the monotonous sound of drumbeats start, I lay down on the couch (sometimes I lie on the floor) and covered my eyes with a bandana. I thought about where the point was located. I began by imagining a large hill in the shape of my own body. I climbed up the hill to my hand and allowed myself to sink into the point, *Joining of the Valleys* . . .

I found myself hiking through the underbrush of a darkening valley. It was twilight, and a half moon peeked over the edge of the mountain range to my right. I was heading up to the pass between the two mountain ranges, to the place where two valleys meet. The animal I relied on paced in front of me. I could hear his breathing and feel his gentle presence, urging me forward. We had someone to meet in that place of neither here nor there, neither one valley nor the other. We were going to meet the spirit of the point.

I didn't know who I would find there; I just knew someone would be waiting. I didn't even know if the spirit would manifest as human or animal, male or female. As we began to climb, occasionally my boot would dislodge a rock and I would hear it roll all the way back down the hill and hit the bottom. It was a little frightening, even though I knew I was where I was supposed to be. My guide told me to hang onto his fur as the climb became even steeper. Finally, we stepped up to the place where all joined - sky, valleys and mountains. A campfire flamed in the very center, and an old man was sitting by it. He looked like an old-time gold-digger or gold-panner from the movies, simmering beans in a beat-up old pot. When he looked up at me, his eyes caught the moonlight and I felt the light penetrate my chest.

"Come sit by the fire, child. I have been waiting for you," he said. "Taste the soup I have made for you." He poured some thick, creamy stuff into a cup and handed it to me.

It tasted salty, (like tears,) filled with chunks of vegetables and grains. There was a strong herbal component, and soon I felt dizzy and fluid. The song of the moon filled me - not just my physical body, but also an area around me. It was as though my capacity to hold light were bigger than my body. The silvery light seemed audible even tangible.

"What would you like to know?" the man asked.

As we talked, his form vibrated and shifted. His white beard looked red or blue at times, while his shape grew larger, then smaller. Sometimes he looked solid; sometimes I could see through him as if he were made of smoke.

"I want to know the medicine of this place, and how to use it for my patients."

He threw a handful of herbs on the fire and a purple smoke formed above the flames. From the haze, a voice spoke:

"In the place that is between form and no-form, a patient's potential is as great as whatever they can imagine. This point, Joining of the Valleys, is an opening; it is a place to remove barriers and bring elements together. When you come to the place of joining, to the very center, where one valley ends and the other begins, it is also a place where mountains join and also the earth and sky. In the center all is joined. The medicine of this place gives unlimited possibilities, and you can return at any time to choose again. Let any stuck-ness flow down the rivers, which also join here and share a source. See the infinite choices that come from the sky to inspire you. All your thoughts and ideas come to join here and flow out of here. Joining of the Valleys is a place where all imposed nos, whether external or internal, can become yeses."

The smoke floated away and the voice stopped. My head cleared. The old man nodded to me and vanished. The fire was gone, leaving not even ash. It was as if the fire had never been. My animal guide and I climbed back down the path, and I became aware of drumbeats calling me back to my physical body. I opened my eyes and breathed in. I knew I would go back to the old man again. Yes I would go often to that place of infinite possibility.

While, I have visited many acupuncture points, this particular point, the one that woke me up years ago in Los Angeles, has been my teacher time and again. Six weeks after that first treatment, I left my husband, left the church, and started a path that has been neither easy nor conventional, yet it is one I was born to. It is the path that called me, and it feels like home.

My village is fluid and the residents come and go. Sometimes I welcome them to sit by my "campfire" and drink the soup that awakens the eyes of healing, and other times I simply offer them the medicine of the ancestors until they awaken in their own time. Many times, my patients and friends are my teachers. We help one another awaken ever more deeply to the place of infinite possibility.

Chapter 2: Lawrence and Very Great Abyss (Lung 9)

It is said in many religious teachings that the sins of the father are passed down from generation to generation, or visited on the sons for seven generations. At the same time, the number seven is often associated with heaven or perfection. I have often puzzled over these teachings. If my great-great-great, etc. grandparents did something bad and it was visited upon their son or daughter, and then the next son or daughter and so on, where does the seventh generation start? I think I have come to believe that in the human race there is darkness, or the capacity to do harm, just as there is light, the capacity to do great things. As for the balance, I am reminded of an ancient story about two wolves. I have done extensive research to find it's author or origin, and as far as I can tell, no one knows it's origin, many say it is Cherokee, but it has also been quoted in Irish literature as two dogs. This is one of the versions I found online:

"Two Wolves

An old Cherokee chief is teaching his grandson about life:

'A fight is going on inside me,' he said to the boy. 'It is a terrible fight and it is between two wolves. One is evil - he is anger, envy, sorrow, regret, greed, arrogance, self-pity, guilt, resentment, inferiority, lies, false pride, superiority, self-doubt, and selfishness.

The other wolf is good - he is joy, peace, love, hope, serenity, humility, kindness, benevolence, empathy, generosity, truth, compassion, and faith. The same fight is going on inside you - and inside every other person, too.'

The grandson thought for a minute and asked his grandfather, 'Which wolf will win?'

The old chief replied, 'The one you feed.'"

_____

When I was studying art at El Camino College, from 1979-1982, I became friends with an African-American man who influenced me greatly. Lawrence was at least 15 years older than I, and we took many of the same classes. He was of the B'Hai faith, a faith of world peace. We would go for coffee after class and spend hours and hours talking, often about the battle for black civil rights. Lawrence lived through those times.

Lawrence had an amazing sense of humor. One day he told me about a time in the early '60s when he went to the movies with a friend. The friend was white, and there were two entrances to the movie theater, one for "coloreds" and one for "whites."

As they were about to enter the door for "whites," they were confronted by an employee who told Lawrence the "colored" entrance was around back. Lawrence looked him in the eye and said, "Well, if I see any of them, I'll let them know." And he got away with it! We laughed so hard I had tears rolling down my face. (Underneath that laughter, of course, lay pain and guilt. No one should be treated the way black people were - and still are all too often.)

I have read about, and seen many movies about the experience of black Americans, and while we have come a long way, we still have a long way to go. The sins of our fathers still live deeply in our souls. Lawrence was quick to tell me that during the era of civil rights marches, there were as many if not more white people marching for black rights as there were black people. I felt heartened by that knowledge, because that's how it should be. The "good" wolf, the one we want to feed, should stand up for all those who need support. In the case of black civil rights, white people could get away with marching more easily than could blacks. They were less likely to be beaten or killed for it, so some of the task of advancing civil rights necessarily fell on whites.

When I was in middle school, in 1970, I lived in an area with a lot of racial tension and went to a predominantly black school. Though my father was in the military and we had moved around a lot, this was my first exposure to black people, let alone black culture. Being sheltered and yet knowing the history, I was very tentative. I didn't want to step on toes or make anyone angry. Well, it was my tentativeness that got me in trouble. The kids made fun of me for being fearfully polite. Eventually, a group of girls decided I was the target and I got picked on and beat up. Each day I was terrified to go to school. In spite of this experience, I don't blame African American people for being angry. Theirs is a righteous anger. They are American citizens, yet they bear an unjust heritage of slavery, torture, bigotry, and all the rest of it.

Atrocities have happened - and still happen - all over the world. Because I am an American, however, the ones I feel most deeply are American. Look at the atrocities our American ancestors visited upon the innocent peoples who lived here before them, - not only the Indian tribes, but also the animals, plants, and the Earth herself. I once visited a mesa called Acoma in New Mexico, just west of Albuquerque, that has been continuously inhabited for more than thirteen hundred years. Its people make amazingly beautiful pottery. I paid to go on a walking tour of the pueblo, led by an Acoma Pueblo tribe member. (The people of Acoma are believed to be descendants of the Anasazi, although anthropologists are not sure.) In the center of the village was a Catholic church. The guide told us that the

Spanish conquerers came into their village and cut off the right foot of every male between the ages of 12 and 25. Just imagine how many died from infections. When it came time to build the church (I still wonder whose foot Jesus would have cut off), the men couldn't build it as they were crippled, so the Spanish forced the women to build the church. I don't understand why the Acomans of today don't burn the church down. I stood there listening to this story with tears flowing at the horror of it. Other tourists were hardly paying attention, and a few were even laughing. As we walked out of the church, the guide came over and put his arm around my shoulders. He quietly said to me, "It's okay, we forgive." Incredible!

Look at the many other atrocities Western culture has perpetrated, that we must never forget. The witch burnings, the holocaust, the unjust treatment of Japanese Americans in WWII, the bombings of Dresden, Nagasaki, Hiroshima, colonialism, later trade agreements as one-sided as the colonial ones, and the list goes on. These are just atrocities against other humans. The modern West has also attacked animals, the myriad species we have brought to extinction or near extinction; the trees whom we murder in order to build new strip malls and grow more biofuels; and the Earth herself, whom we rape and poison daily.

Lawrence disappeared one semester and I was never able to find him again. He was in my life for only a short while, but long enough to teach me much about love and human dignity. I am reminded of a Bible verse, "Forget not to show love unto strangers: for thereby some have entertained angels unawares." (Hebrews 13:2) Lawrence was my angel.

Very Great Abyss - The Journey

I start the drumming CD and lie down with my eyes covered. The point is located on the inner surface of the arm, about an inch from the wrist crease on the inside of the arm below the thumb. As I slip into the journey state, I find the point and sink in, then feel myself falling into a dark pool of water. There seems to be no bottom: I keep falling and falling and falling. (Being in non-ordinary reality, I am able to breathe.) Finally, the movement stops. When I look up to see what has happened, I find that I am in a very large fishing net held by an Octopus, who is laughing at my confusion. I ask if he is the spirit of the point and he says "No." So I ask why he is holding me in a net. He laughs once again and carries the net, with me still in it, down the street. I can see now that we are passing through an underwater city, complete with streetlights, buildings, mailboxes and fire hydrants (which seems a bit unnecessary). As we near the edge of the city the Octopus dumps me out onto the street, where a man is standing beside a ledge that drops down sharply. No bottom can be seen. He is dressed in blue jeans and a flannel plaid shirt. He has hiking boots, and his backpack is sitting on the ground next to him. He looks about 50 years old with salt and pepper hair and clear blue eyes.

The man turns to me and says, "You know, you could just fall and fall forever." I ask if he is the spirit of the point, and he says, "Yes."

"What do you mean, I could just fall and fall forever?"

"Just when you think you have gone as deep as you can, you find you can go deeper." He smiles and takes a deep breath. Pointing out into the cavernous abyss, he says, "You probably thought that "Very Great Abyss," was more about grief, didn't you?"

"Yes."

He holds out his hand to me and together we jump over the ledge. As we fall further and further, colder and darker, I see flashes of things I have lost in my life. Pets, friends, family . . . Then I begin to see human history going by - wars, massacres, slavery, destruction of the planet. I realize I am crying. Then we see ancient civilizations, people of Rome, Egypt, Babylon, Mesopotamia, and China, people who lived at the whim of Empires. Finally we see the most ancient people, hunters and gatherers of every color, people who lived in nomadic tribes or villages. Here I feel a fluttering in my heart and my chest expand. I call this feeling joy.

When we finally land, we are no longer in water. I am lying on a grassy hillside, in the blazing warmth of sunlight.

As I breathe deeply, the man says to me, "All of the visions live inside you and everyone else." He goes on, "The abyss can be difficult to look at because you will want to say it was someone else who did these things. "It couldn't be me?." But it could. You have the capacity for darkness. All humans do, and once you allow yourself to see that, you can see in a new way that you also have the capacity to live in the light. All humans do. You can forgive and move forward into a world beyond them"s" verses us"es". When enough people move forward, the world will change.

"Your friend, Lawrence, grew up as a black man in a bigoted society. He went deeply into his spirituality and his art. He embraced the understanding of oneness, which allowed him to live with integrity. He could laugh and live a life of grace. That state is what this point offers."

He continues, "Jumping off the ledge into the abyss changes us forever, and that change allows us to hold all things sacred, fascinating, and perfect exactly the way they are. All things have happened by a larger design and had to happen exactly the way they have. Everything that happens - <u>everything</u> - is part of the oneness experiencing itself through you. Take your patients to the abyss when they are caught up in the conversation of darkness versus light, or 'them versus us,' or the grief of unbearable loss. The abyss will remind them how big the picture really is, and that everything has a purpose and perfect design."

I thank him and ride the drumbeats back to ordinary reality, my mind still reeling with all that I saw in the abyss. I pick up my laptop to record the journey.

It's interesting, as I have always thought of an abyss as a bad thing. A hole with no end, an emotion that strangles me forever. Reframing abyss to the big picture is helpful, and in that bigness I can see it as a place of deep understanding and possibility. The potential for offering this point to patients who are viewing their life with a small mind, and helping them open up to greater possibilities, thrills me.

Chapter 3: Leslie and Arnie - Side Passage: (Large Intestines 6)

When I was in acupuncture school in Florida, one of my classmates, Leslie, started dating a man who was dying from cancer of the throat and brain. This man, Arnie, had studied classical five-element acupuncture with J.R. Worsley in England and he taught the one and only course on five-element acupuncture at the Santa Fe acupuncture school, where Leslie had been a student. Inspired by Arnie's class, she moved to Florida, to study at the Worsley Institute of Classical Acupuncture.

Meanwhile, Arnie was diagnosed with cancer and moved back home to Florida, where he started assisting at the school. He and Leslie then reconnected and became a couple. In the summer of 1991, our class went to England to study for a month and Arnie came with us. He was not doing well by this time. The pain in his head was so severe he couldn't sleep, even morphine could barely touch the pain.

One morning in the student kitchen, I asked Leslie how she was doing. She replied, "I am in love with a man who is dying of cancer. I fell in love with him knowing he was dying. We don't have time to fight about the little things, so it is lovely and bittersweet and fucked up all at once. People have criticized me for even entering this relationship, but when love comes to you, you must follow it."

Her words inspired me to write a poem for her and Arnie.

Here it is:

> Choose we risks?
> We choose to take.
> And in the risks
> we embrace the pain.
> Birth and life and love
> are seeded with the risk.
> We choose to embrace
> the risk in these.
> The greater the risk:
> the higher the reward,
> the deeper the love,
> the more intense the pain,
> the less focused the trivialities.
> Plant your seed
> deep within my soul
> and in your pain, my pain
> one moment, eternal
> love grows.
> And the risk
> is worth
> the take.

Our class had a propensity to sing that had emerged sometime in our first year, when a number of us used to eat lunch sprawled out in the grass by a canal behind the school. One day a couple of students started singing, and then the rest joined in, and from then on we sang. We even created a book of our favorite folk songs. One of them, "My love is like a red, red rose" (by Robbie Burns), was special to Arnie, so the class got together and taped it, harmonies and all, for him to play when he needed to hear it.

Leslie and Arnie left England several weeks early so he could be more comfortable, and when class reconvened in November, Arnie was barely alive. Leslie would come to school each morning not sure he'd be alive in the evening. On the day he died, his sister called Leslie and told her to come, but Arnie died before she got home. She was able to spend time alone with his body and hold him.

Several days later, Leslie and I were sitting by the canal when I again asked how she was doing. She said that in many ways Arnie's death had been a relief, because he'd been so sick and in such terrible pain. Now she could let him go and move on with her life, as he would want her to do.

Their relationship had lasted for less than a year, a time so intense that in my mind's eye I see them arm and arm for eternity.

This experience was a great learning for me. A gem, which was stated by one of our classmates in England: "Arnie needs to decide how he wants to live the rest of his life." Then she added, "And that is what we *all* need to do, moment by moment, as all of us are dying." Putting this thought together with Leslie's words about not having the time to fight over the little things, I began to realize that *none* of us have the time to fight over the little things. None of us know when death will come - it might be today. Why taint our lives with pettiness? I am so grateful that Leslie and Arnie had the courage to love each other, even knowing how short their time would be. Their story reminds me to always part from my loved ones with kind and loving words.

Side Passage - The Journey

I enter the point on the edge of my forearm, about three inches up the arm from the wrist crease, on the thumb side, as the drumbeats from the CD bring on the familiar state of consciousness, after sinking into the point, I find myself dropping onto a mountain ledge. The sun is hot on my shoulders, and after I look down I want to huddle back against the rock:

birds are flying below me! Why the drop must be hundreds of feet! Above me, only more ledges - and the ledge I am on is blocked by a boulder the size of a city bus. I am alone in the sky with no way to move along the ledge.

I am scared of heights in ordinary reality, but here I am mostly perplexed. Which way to go? I walk towards the boulder, wondering if somehow I can shift it, when someone says, "Psst! Here!" I turn to see a crevice in the rock wall, just large enough that I can squeeze through. When I do, a short man stands in the crevice beckoning me to follow. So I follow.

He is a peculiar little man about five feet tall, with curly red hair who is graying at the temples. He wears a plaid shirt and khaki beige shorts that come just below his knees, set off by multi-colored athletic shoes. He looks back to make sure I am following and I can see he has little round spectacles on the tip of his nose, round rosy cheeks, and a slight grin.

We move through the stony passage and up a few steps and I find myself back on the ledge, but past the boulder. Seeing my surprise, he laughs.

"Are you the spirit of this point?" I ask.

"Yes. I help you to move from one level to the next. You must know that when you can't go any farther with something, and so you think you might be stuck, it is best to let go of your expectations. Just take the side passage. It is there that you - or your patients - will find an energy that impels you to the next cycle or level in life."

We walk for a while in silence. The vista is breath-taking. I look out across a green valley with a small river running through the center. There are goats and deer grazing in lush grass. In the distance there are majestic snow caps. The wind is blowing a chilled breeze all the way from those mountains, and farther yet I can make out the shimmering blue of an ocean, its white foamy caps parading toward the sand. The air smells sweet from wild flowers that bloom all over the hillsides, and I notice that my fear of heights is absent. I am lost in my wonder at the world.

"All things have their time," says my companion. "Nothing stays the same. Many people come to the boulders that signify the end of a cycle and they can't see any way to move on. They sit down by their boulder and wish that life would stay the same. In short, they have spiritual and emotional constipation. This point, Side Passage, will help them find a way past the obstacle to the start of something new. Life goes on."

At the top of the mountain we find a small field of very soft grass, where goats are grazing. We sit down and bask in the warm sunlight. The grass has a tang of peppermint.

"How can people go on when they lose someone they love?" I ask. "It always seems way too soon."

"it is appropriate to sit a while by the the boulder and grieve what could have been."

He smiles at me, and I notice he has bright green eyes and freckles. "At some point, however, one needs nourishment and refreshment, and then it's time to leave the boulder. The time is different for everyone. If you offer this point before the person is ready to move, the point will show them the possibility. If they are ready, Side Passage will ease them into movement."

I thank him and ask the best way to get off the mountain. He grins and takes me to the other side, where there is a water slide that must be five miles high, going from the peak all the way to the ground. I laugh, too. This will be <u>fun</u>!

"Are you ready?" he asks.

I sit down at the top of the slide and say yes. He gives me a shove and I ride down and down and down, screaming, hair blowing all the way, till I land in a lake at the bottom. My totem animal is waiting and brings me back to ordinary reality.

As I think about this journey, I wonder how many "side passages" I have missed when I thought I was stuck, and how many have I taken without even realizing it. It occurs to me that stuck-ness is a choice, sometimes as the spirit said, appropriate for a time, and that movement is also a choice. I am reminded of a piece of wisdom I often tell patients who are afraid to move in their lives - afraid of making the wrong decision. I say to them "it's much harder to turn the steering wheel on a stopped car, but when the car is moving, you can turn in any direction with ease."

Section 2: Winter

I love winter almost as much as autumn. I love snow days when all the busy, busy world turns off. It's like a gift of time, a day free of plans and commitments. I love to stay home, make a batch of soup, and sit by the fire with a book. My cats and dog curl up beside me and we snuggle in. I also love the holidays of winter: Thanksgiving, Solstice, Christmas, and New Year's. Winter is the time of year when families gather and create traditions around food, gifts and loving hospitality. I also love to play in the snow and make cool snowmen, then dress them up with scarves and hats.

Most of the mammals on the planet hibernate in winter - except the two-leggeds. The very first winter I lived in Maryland as an adult was 1995-6, when in early January, just after New Year's, we had a blizzard -- truly a blizzard: We got three feet of snow. I had just moved into my new house, but my family was still in South Florida, and the furniture hadn't arrived, so there I was in an empty house, all by myself. I did have a snow shovel, food, several books, and a good example: The next door neighbor was out shoveling his driveway every few hours, so I figured that's what you're supposed to do. I did it too. Then when I came in, I was exhausted and I slept for hours and hours. Puzzling . . . I couldn't figure out why I was so tired! Really, shoveling wasn't all that hard. . . In years to come, as I felt that same tiredness wash over me every winter, snow storms or not, I realized that my body had been adjusting to the downward energy of the Maryland winter. It hadn't been that way in summery Florida.

The ancient Chinese counseled that winter is the time to go deep - hibernate, reflect, dream, be quiet, and generally rest up before the growing season comes again, and our bodies seem to agree. Yet patients come to me all the time in the winter and say they are depressed, or have "seasonal affective disorder." When I ask into it, very few seem actually depressed. They are not in despair or even near despair. Forced to get specific, the worst symptoms most can cite are being tired all the time and wanting to stay in bed. Once I'm sure that's the issue, I usually tell them to listen to their bodies and sleep as much as they want. Oh, the silliness of the human race, wanting to act like it's summer in the winter. The pharmaceutical industry loves us for it.

The emotion for winter - don't forget, these labels are translations of translations from the ancient Chinese texts - is said to be "fear," another word that is only the tip of an iceberg. Modern Americans tend to think fear is bad, but that's not so. Indeed, appropriate fear is a driving force for survival. It can serve as a wake-up call - "Hmm, something's off. I think I won't go after all." "Fear" also gives us the wisdom to make sure we have what we need to make it through the winter, and the caution to conserve resources till the spring. You could call that fear, or you could call it the will to live. I think fear is an aspect of our very deep genetic programming to persevere for life, for the next generations, for the continuance of all that matters.

The religious tradition of Lent lives on from an ancient time when resources at the end of winter would be running low, while the first plants of spring would not be ready for a few more weeks. It seems to me, no coincidence that people gave something up "to God" in a way and at a time that conserved whatever stored food was left. This sacrifice was for the good of all, so that life could continue.

The organs (or officials) for this season are the Bladder and the Kidneys, which store and process the essence of life - the waters. No surprise - the element of the winter is Water.

The next time we experience winter, let's give in to our bodies' desire to sleep and rest. Don't be too quick to label it "depression." Rather, be glad that our bodies are so smart that they observes the life rhythm that all other mammals do in winter.

Chapter 4: Fear of Death: Dark Gate (Kidney 21)

Death is a part of life - often the part of life we avoid discussing and sometimes *even thinking* about. Having grown up in a semi-fundamentalist Christian household, I was indoctrinated to see death as the enemy: the last enemy Christ would conquer. As a child I learned the prayer, "Now I lay me down to sleep, I pray the lord my soul to keep. And if I die before I wake, I pray the lord my soul to take." That prayer scared me to my core: I didn't want to die before I woke.

I also remember a book of children's Christian stories in the dentist's office that I used to read while my siblings and I waited to get our teeth cleaned. In one story, a little boy was hit by a car and taken to the hospital. A nurse explained to the boy that Jesus walks through the hospital at night to heal the boys and girls, and that if he keeps his arm up, Jesus will see him. The boy was too weak to hold his arm up, so the nurse propped it up with a pillow. When Jesus came through that night, he saw the boy's arm and took him along. Thus the boy dies! Of course, that story scared me too.

Do you remember the Bible verse that says, "Don't let the sun go down on your wrath"? In my childhood household that verse was taken to mean that if you had an argument with someone, you'd better settle it before you went to bed. Otherwise, one of you might die in your sleep, and then you'd never be able to work it out. I remember that as a teenager -- a turbulent time for many parents and kids -- I was sometimes up half the night because we couldn't sleep till we settled our quarrel. I would be told again that one of us might die in our sleep and whoever was still alive would feel horrible if our last interaction was a fight. I was headstrong and stubborn and so were they, so the arguments went on and on and on.

This fearful teaching around death was buried for a while in my subconscious, until I became a senior in high school and got involved with a Christian cult. After graduation, I let them talk me out of going straight to college. Instead, I joined their outreach program and was sent to Los Angeles. The teachings of this group further increased my fears: they taught us that Satan was unable to read our minds, so we should never express our fears out loud or Satan would bring them to pass. That's how I learned to stuff my fears and speak only positive things, regardless of whether I actually believed or felt them. Now, there is some value in thinking and speaking the positive. Suppressing fears and negative thoughts without examination, however, is like sewing up a dirty wound. Even if the surface heals, infection can fester underneath.

Eventually I left the cult and joined a fundamentalist Christian church in California, which at first felt like freedom - at least compared to the cult. I got married and had my first daughter eleven months later. So at age 23, almost 24, I became a stay-at-home mom, and I also came to know a young woman in the church who was dying from breast cancer that had spread to her brain. To make it worse, she had small children -- like me. In addition, my best friend's sister was also dying of cancer. In the presence of these dying friends, my old fear of death surfaced like a sea monster that had been waiting to attack.

Kapow! Every bump or mark on my body looked to me like cancer, and every time I went to bed, I lay there trembling because I was sure I was going to have a heart attack and die in my sleep. But I still could not speak my fear -- not even to my husband. After a while the fear got so bad that I hardly slept for nights on end, until I would finally "konk" out for a night out of sheer exhaustion. I'd lie there with my heart racing, hardly able to breathe, and then I would imagine my left arm or shoulder aching. Or sometimes I'd roam the house, but mostly I lay in bed with my eyes shut, pretending to sleep so "Satan wouldn't know my fears".

Once I tried to talk to my best friend about this fear and her response was, "You're a Christian, you know where you'll go. Why should *you* be afraid of death?" I felt shamed. "She was right," I thought. If I really loved Jesus, I shouldn't be afraid to go to heaven! Therefore, my fear must be my own fault, a weakness in my faith. Then another friend's sister committed suicide, and because she hadn't been a Christian, my friend was devastated. She kept saying her sister was burning in hell. I continued stuffing my fears and walking the house at night. My husband was oblivious to my suffering. He just slept right through everything.

After our second daughter was born, the fears escalated until death seemed everywhere. I spent days begging God not to let me die so I could be there for my daughters. Every time I got in an airplane, I begged God not to let it crash. I was a wreck and I couldn't tell anyone.

When I started having acupuncture, many things shifted for me. My acupuncturist was a Jewish man who practiced Sufism and lived in a community of people who called themselves a mystical school. My Christian friends thought I was foolish to engage with a non-believer in this way, as I would talk with my acupuncturist about my beliefs and ask him about his. He was very respectful of my beliefs. He was one of the kindest people I have ever met. I have to admit that I had a crush on him, in part because he <u>was</u> so kind and good. He loved his wife and daughter, he did things for his community, and he was deeply spiritual. I started to question that a person like him would burn in hell after death. After all, he was just as devout in his beliefs as I was in mine. So I started to entertain the possibility that God was bigger than just one religion. I'm sure this new openness was why my Christian friends didn't want me to get acupuncture treatments.

While my fear of death did not go away, it did subside for a while, only to re-emerge a few years later when I was in Acupuncture school. My belief system had broadened considerably by then, and at school I was surrounded by New Age thinkers. When my fear of death reared its ugly head, however, the New Agers were no more helpful than my Christian friends. They said things like, "Why would you be afraid, death is just transcending from one plane to the next," or "You just go on to your next life." Oh dear, obviously, I wasn't as spiritual as these wise ones! What was <u>wrong</u> with me? My fear was now so severe that I couldn't be around anyone who was dying — in itself a problem for a health practitioner, let alone that I suffered. If I even heard talk about anyone who was dying or had died, I'd once more be up all night. Fear was itself my disease (dis-ease).

Then - What luck! - I had a miracle healing from a guest teacher, the author of a book that marries shamanism and acupuncture with plants. He is an acupuncturist, herbalist, and shaman who has trained with the Hiechol tribe in Mexico. He taught our class how to do a shamanic journey, and he offered to give each of us a plant spirit healing. One by one, we each went up to the front of the class where he took our pulses, asked us briefly what was going on, and gave us one or several plant spirits. Then he took our pulses again and sent us on our way. (In Chinese medicine there are twelve pulses, six on each wrist. They are central to assessing the state of a person's energy [Qi] and to knowing when a treatment is complete.)

When it was my turn, I was uneasy about being in front of the class on a treatment table. He asked me why I was trembling and I said I was nervous. He matter-of-factly took my pulses and put something under my tongue. Then he looked me in the eye and spoke right to my soul. "What are you *really* afraid of?" The word "death" tumbled out of my mouth before I even knew it was coming. I was mortified. I thought, now everyone knows what I'm afraid of. But the teacher just said, "Oh." He put something else under my tongue, took my pulses, and said, "That's it."

I didn't feel any different, so I didn't give the episode any thought until about three months later, when it dawned on me that I no longer spent my nights in trembling fear. What's more, I could think about death with no emotional charge whatsoever. It was amazing, and to this day, all these years later, I have never again feared death. I have worked with dying people, visited people in hospice, and even participated in an exercise that gave us a near-death experience, and I have felt no fear.

I don't know what plant spirits the teacher gave me that day or how it worked, and I never did any prolonged psychotherapy around this fear. It just evaporated, a miracle as great to me as being cured of cancer would have been. It was this profound healing that propelled me to study shamanism after I had finished acupuncture school.

Dark Gate - The Journey

As the drum beats, from the drum I am playing, help me to alter my consciousness, I go to my chest about an inch and a half from the center, at the bottom of the rib cage, and sink into the point. I am in darkness slowly falling through something that feels like thick liquid until I land with a thud. My power animal is instantly at my side, and I look up to see a large wrought-iron gate. It has black spikes and spider webs; rather like the gate in front of the *Addam's Family* house in the 1960s sitcom. Suddenly, the gate creaks open, I walk in with my animal, and it slams shut on my heels. It feels creepy. I look around and see a smallish woman sitting on the ground just inside the gate. She wears a dark grey, mid-calf dress with three quarter length sleeves. It is difficult to tell her age as her face is stark white, with dark circles under her eyes. She has long black hair that is blowing in the cold breeze. The oddest thing about her is that she is laughing like a hyena.

I ask, "What is so funny?"

She says, "You are. You should have seen the look on your face when the gate slammed shut."

Now she is actually rolling around on the ground, holding her stomach with tears of laughter rolling down her face. I can't help but laugh too, though I feel confused, and my power animal is also laughing. My logical brain thinks: This is really strange. Dark Gate is a point on a Water meridian, and laughter is associated with Fire. What's up? Did I do something wrong? As soon as the thought forms, the woman stops laughing and says emphatically, "Nothing is wrong!"

She stands up. She is about up to my chin - and I'm not tall - but she has a very big presence. Power hits me like a tidal wave as she looks me in the eye.

"Sit down," she commands, and I do. The ground is hard and there isn't any lawn, only patches of dirt and occasional sprigs of crab grass and weeds. The old house behind her is boarded up. When the wind blows, a few shingles that are hanging by one nail rattle against the house.

"Why are you here?" Again the force of the ocean is behind her voice and words.

"I am looking for the spirit of Dark Gate to ask for its medicine and how to use this point for my patients."

"WELL! You're looking at her." She sits down directly in front of me. "When your patients have come through a dark time in their lives, don't you think a little laughter might help? My gate will help when they are ready to move out of darkness. By that I don't mean when all their problems are gone, but just that they are ready to take the next step. Offering my medicine to them gives them the gentle push they need. The gate is a bit scary, so you know that my medicine gives courage." She speaks quickly, word tumbling after word, taking breaths in odd places like in the middle of the word medicine: medi - (breath) - cine.

She turns toward the house behind her and waves her arm. Instantly, the house is transformed into a beautiful Victorian showpiece. The paint is fresh, the shingles in place, and the glass of the door and windows sparkle. I notice that I am sitting in lush grass.

She jumps up, like water being shot from a squirt gun, and begins to dance around me, singing a song that sounds like a bubbling fountain. The sound is so beautiful that I am moved to tears. Then she stops dancing and places her hands on the top of my head, a gesture that feels like a warm shower. I feel fears melting from me and being offered to the ground.

"When you use this point, let your patients know that the warm water will help their darknesses become gifts to Mother Earth," she says. "The dry, barren landscape of their lives can be transformed into fertile ground and beauty if they dare walk through the gate." She kisses the top of my head. "Now take your animal and go." She blends into the gate and is gone. The gate swings open for me to leave. I return to myself on the waves of the drum beats.

I put my drum down and think about this point. Facing fear and walking through it, leads us to a better place. The better place is within us. When my fear left, after speaking it out loud to the shaman, I could think about death in a different way. I could be of service to the dying, and thus to the living.

Chapter 5: Peace in Chaos: Fly and Scatter (Bladder 58)

When I was ten years old, I had a dream that I still remember in detail. In the dream, the whole world was fighting and people lay dying on every side. I did not join the fight. As I watched, the fighters ran out of ammunition and began throwing rocks and using their guns as clubs. I went with some folks into a cave, on the side of a mountain, to hide. We had to step over bodies, a few still moving, to reach the caves. We waited there, until finally after some days, there was only silence outside. We all walked out of the caves, past the bodies, and down the sides of several mountains, to a very large amphitheater with a movie screen. As we sat there in stillness, the word GOD appeared on the screen.

I had many similar dreams over the years of growing up and in my young adulthood. In the dreams I am never involved in the fighting, I always survive, and quite often I end up tending the sick and injured. Having grown up in a conservative Christian household, I always assumed these dreams reflected the stories I'd heard about the coming "end times," or "apocalypse," or "the tribulation" -- the predicted hell on earth after God takes up all the Christians into heaven. I always wondered why I stayed there helping people, however. Why was I not in heaven with the others? If the others were indeed in heaven?

Now I have a different view of these dreams, one that began to coalesce on September 11, 2001. I was living near Washington D.C. by now, and I was on the treadmill at my gym with a TV screen right in front of me, where I watched the planes crash into the World Trade center. Even though they showed it again and again, I could hardly believe my eyes. Then I went home and turned on the TV only to hear about the Pentagon. Was there more to come? No, no . . . It couldn't be true. These things don't happen in America!

Dazed, I made sure my daughters were okay and got ready for work. I had a full day of patients, and I figured they would all cancel, but I had to be there anyway. To my surprise, however, every single one showed up. They were traumatized and needed me to take care of them, using one or another of the restorative treatments for an injured spirit that are preserved in Five Element acupuncture. As I went through the day, I kept having a sensation of deja vu. I felt I'd done this before - but of course I hadn't. Only towards the end of the day did I remember my dreams.

Then I realized that days like this one, were what I was here for. The dreams had been sent to let me know that God was always with me, that I would be okay, and that my path in life was to help people who needed tending in difficult times.

On the news, that evening, I watched the towers collapse over and over, over and over. I listened to the taped conversation between the woman on the plane that hit the Pentagon and her husband, thinking about that being their last conversation. I thought about the desperate people who jumped from the towers, and the ones who talked to their loved ones knowing there was no way out. I admired the courage and resourcefulness of the group who gained control of the hijackers and crashed the plane in Pennsylvania. They were willing to die to save a building full of others. All evening I heard jets patrolling, as well as the eerie silence of the skies between their patrols. In the midst of this horror I had the strongest sense, that I have ever experienced in my life, of who I am and what I am called to do.

In the days that followed, I treated a D.C. policewoman who had been on duty the day of the attacks, at the heart of the city's fear and chaos. I treated a young mother so panicked that she moved away from the area, for the safety of her children. I had treated her for years, and then she was gone. I treated people who worked for the NSA, and others who were in the military. Everyone had a story, and everyone needed to tell their story, and I saw that I was able to maintain my center and calm. Then I started treating postal workers who were all on antibiotics for possible exposure to anthrax. I treated a man who was in a job so top-secret he never could tell me what he did or where he worked.

I knew that this was what I was here for. This was my calling, and Spirit had been preparing me since I was small. Tragic though it all was, I felt a strange satisfaction because I knew in my bones that I was in the right place at the right time, and I knew I could help.

Watching TV one night, I saw thousands of New Yorkers gathered at Ground Zero with candles, singing. At first I thought it was sad that it took a tragedy to bring these people together, and then I was filled with hope and joy that in the midst of the tragedy people could join together despite differences of color, religion, beliefs, political affiliation, etc. and hold hands, light candles and sing. It reminded me of *The Grinch who Stole Christmas,* by Dr. Seuss a book and movie in which the evil Grinch stole the whole town's trees, trimmings, presents - he stole Christmas, as the title declares, yet, on Christmas morning the townspeople gather and sing. The Grinch learned that he could only steal *things*: he could not steal the love and spirit that is Christmas. It is the same with the 9/11 terrorists, who thought they could blast the heart of Wall Street and break the American spirit. But they could not. They could not, because the human spirit is greater than we could ever have imagined. Unfortunately, it often takes tragedy for that spirit to shine forth.

The world as we know it may in fact be about to end. The oceans are becoming too warm and too acidic, and the climate is eratic, while pollution, pesticides, and droughts are killing both us and our Mother Earth. Yet, I still believe there are those of us who are here, for a purpose, in the right place and at the right time. Yes, the rich are getting richer, but when the poor and working class can no longer serve, what good will their money do them?

At a farmer's market recently, I saw many, many people selling meats that were local, uncaged or free range, and free of hormones, insecticides, and herbicides. There were recycled arts and products. Soaps, lotions, and clothing made locally. There is a movement toward sustainability, and it may be starting slow, but it is moving. It is gaining momentum. There will be many ways to survive and be happy with much, much less material possessions, and I believe we are here at this time and place to make it happen, for the sake of the children (who are our future).

Think of it this way: Even if it really is too late to preserve a planet we can live on, what harm will it do to try? If we give up hope, we create a self-fulfilling prophesy of doom.

I once took a shamanic journey far into the future, because I wanted to talk with a descendant of mine to see how things turned out. I found myself about a thousand years in the future, where/when my descendant was a middle aged man. Both walls and floors of his home were made of hardwood. The doors and windows were all open and I could see food growing on every inch of ground. I noticed a little robotic thing moving over the floors and up the walls, continuously cleaning. I asked my descendant to explain the open doors and windows. How was it safe, and what kept bugs from coming in? He said that an inaudible frequency of sound waves bounced back and forth between the door and window frames, (like a force field), which insects disliked and wouldn't cross. As for crime, he said that no one bothered anyone else's home, because they all had everything they needed. It looked like paradise to me. He told me that I had been instrumental in the way things were for him and everyone else on the planet.

Me?! Instrumental? He told me that because of my vision for a Council of Trees, the world's entire social/legal/economic structure was set up to speak with the spirits of Nature and gain their approval before doing or building anything. Once Nature was seen in her rightful place, she had rewarded the world with abundance beyond imagination. He then took me to his bookshelf and showed me the books I had written: I couldn't tell how many, but I could see this one very clearly and could see my name on several more - I think I wasn't meant to know how many. He urged me to make sure I fulfill my promise to write, and we parted with a long, warm hug.

I am sure not only that I am where I am supposed to be, but also that the chaos of this time will not break us.

Fly and Scatter - the journey

Once again I put on the drumming CD and lie down, eyes covered, allowing my mind to still. I am on my way to meet the spirit of Fly and Scatter. I enter the point on the outer side of my leg, halfway between the end of the knee crease and my ankle bone. I feel myself falling, then land in the middle of a chaotic hell. I am on a large green field where people are running every which way, so frantic and heedless that I am almost trampled. They are screaming, shouting and cursing. I see blood and people colliding with each other and trampling small children and the elderly. Someone grabs me from behind and lifts me into a horse-drawn carriage, where I meet a man who can only be a prince. He is dressed much like the royalty at a Renaissance Festival, complete with shiny leather boots. He is also very handsome, with deep brown eyes and long eye lashes and a very serious expression. His dark eye brows are furrowed.

"What is happening?" I ask.

"The city is under attack," he says. "My people don't know where to go or what to do, so they are harming one another in their panic."

"Are you the spirit of this point?" I ask.

"Yes, and I am about to show you what I can do."

He steps out of the carriage and holds up a huge horn, which he blows loudly three times. The sound is so loud I can hear it echoing from the hills surrounding what I now see is a valley with a village. When he stops, my ears keep on ringing. All the people stop in their tracks and turn towards the Prince.

"My people," he shouts loudly. "Gather yourselves to the center and sit." The people do so.

"Do you see, our attackers are gone? Their number was few, many fewer than you. You are harming yourselves much more than they did, by your panic. Do not fear, my soldiers are trapping the attackers as I speak. Tend your neighbors and loved ones, clean up the mess, and return to your homes."

The people calmly stood and began to help each other. The Prince got back in the carriage and said, "This point helps to calm the scattered and bring a sense of peace in the village."

I return to myself and turn off the CD player.

This journey puzzled me. The name "Fly and Scatter" made me think that the point would scatter something that we would want to get rid of, and yet in my journey everyone was already flying and scattering, and the point got their attention so they could calm down. I could use this point when my patients were frantic or out of control, to help then regain a sense of order.

Chapter 6: White Feather: Walking on the Verandah (Kidney 22)

"Knock on wood", I have never been seriously ill. Oh, I've had flus and colds and viruses. I have had babies. I have felt that I was about to die, though in reality I knew I would get better. I cannot imagine how it might feel to be seriously ill, or to know that while you have good days, they will be ever fewer and farther apart, and that the rest of your life will be painful.

I have had friends who have had life threatening illnesses. One who is mentioned in this book who passed away, and another, not in this book, who had a miraculous healing. There are stories I have read about people who have survived serious illness and gotten better just as they had one step through death's door. Some say that they never gave up the fight and attribute that to their healing. Others say they had to let go and embrace death, and learn what death had to teach them before they got better. I have met folks who fought until the last minute and died anyway. My former talk therapist let go and embraced death, and died. It seems there is no formula. We all have our own lessons, our own initiations, our own battles, and our own miracles.

Some people suffer from mental illnesses such as bi-polar disorder, or serious clinical depression, or agoraphobia or even schizophrenia. There are no known cures for these illnesses, though some medications help.

In traditional shamanism, illness can be physical, mental, emotional or other. The "other" includes things like bad crops, bad luck, disharmony in the home or community, poor hunting, etc. When I think about folks who don't know where their next meal is coming from, or don't have a change of clothes, I must admit, that would feel like illness to me too.

If we look at the word disease and put a hyphen in the word to say dis-ease, then considering anything that is not ease, as illness, makes sense. And some things that are not considered by modern medicine as illness, are still life threatening. Certainly not having food or clean water to drink is life threatening.

I have always had my needs met. I have a place to live, food to eat, and clean water to drink. I have plenty of clothes, and I even get to take trips. Yet, compared to my siblings, I don't make very much money, so I have often felt inadequate. There have been many times when I just made enough money to pay my bills, in the nick of time, for which I am very grateful. However, I've been in a place where most decisions are made by, "can I afford this?" There have been many times when I was anxious enough for my sleep to be disturbed, over finances. I'm sure there are probably a lot of readers who can relate. I would never have seen a financial planner, because they probably would have laughed.

So, we could considered this a long term, potentially life threatening dis-ease.

A few years ago I was at one of Sandra Ingerman's teachers gatherings out west. This particular group I am part of, meet every few years. The retreat center had levels of lodging, and of course, I chose the least expensive. I had plenty of time to save for it. Some of my dearest friends in this group usually stay in the most expensive lodging, and they choose the rooms so they can be together. This particular retreat, the center made a huge mistake. They double booked our group with another group. Check in was pure chaos! The least expensive folks got put in very, very rustic housing, way below the quality of the rooms I had stayed in before, at this center. When I got to my room, which I was supposed to be sharing with someone I didn't know well, I was astounded at how small it was. Barely large enough for the two beds, no dressers, no closet, no chair. I didn't know where I was going to put my stuff. I decided to lie down and ask spirit for help. I asked that there would be no roommate and I could use the other bed for my stuff. After envisioning it the best I could, I laughed at myself and then said to spirit, "I'm here to learn, not to live in luxury, so I let this go." A little while later my roommate showed up and we joked about the accommodations. The bathroom was in another building, so, I slept the first night there (getting up 3 times to go outside to go to the bathroom).

The next day at breakfast, I found out my friends from the expensive lodging were having a battle with the center because, while they were given comparable housing, they had all been split up. They went to the office after breakfast to have it out with the administration. They were given this amazingly beautiful house, out on the land, behind a locked gate. It slept around 15 people. The administration told them they could invite all their friends there, so, low and behold, they invited me to stay there with them. I accepted the offer and ended up in a room, with no roommate. It had a queen bed, a dresser, a closet and an extra chair. I was delighted. I went around thanking spirit all day. What a gift!

The following day I was given an envelope from the center. I was afraid they would tell me I couldn't stay there because it wasn't comparable to what I paid for, but when I opened the envelope I found a refund check for what I paid, given to me for the "inconvenience of having to move"! Spirit blew me away! Never in my wildest dreams had I expected this. I had a wonderful time with my friends and in the beauty of the place. I felt "ease" in my body.

Midway through the week we were told to do a shamanic journey, to look for a spirit teacher associated with the land, and ask for guidance. In my journey, I was climbing over large rocks when I noticed the spirit of a very old Native American. He had waist length white hair, and lot of white feathers attached to his hair. I followed him for a while, climbing higher and over more rocks. Eventually, he went into a very large cave. He had a fire going in the cave, and he sat down beside it. As soon as I entered the cave, he pointed at me and started laughing.

I smiled, and asked, "what's so funny."

"You are," he said, as he stopped laughing. His eyes were twinkling like the stars. He had white skins for clothes. There were many implements dangling from his waist tie, which clinked and clanked when he sat down and rolled around laughing.

"Who are you," I was giggling a bit now, because the laughter had been so infectious.

"My name is White Feather," he said, and then he looked me in the eye and asked, "How'd you like those accommodations you got?"

"I love them, did you have something to do with that?" I asked.

"Nope, but why don't you live your life like that?"

There was a lot more in the conversation, but that question was like an arrow to my heart, or a needle to the right acupuncture point. White Feather has remained a guide for me ever since this time, and he always reminds me that abundance is within my grasp. For me, healing this dis-ease came from letting go, and being grateful for what I had, as well as acknowledging my purpose in being there. When I let go and choose gratitude, there is "ease" in my body, I sleep well, I know all will be taken care of. This was a miraculous healing for me!

Walking on the Verandah - the journey

On this day, I decided to lie down on the couch, not the floor, and I turned on the CD player with the drumbeats. In my vision, I go to the ribcage. This point is located about an inch and a half from the center and on the level of where the sternum meets the xiphoid process, (the little piece of cartilage that hangs down from the center) and I find myself looking down a dark tunnel. I step into the tunnel, which turns out to be so slippery and steep that I lose my footing and slide out of control, faster and faster, till I land with a thud in a mud puddle. When I stand up, the mud turns out to be quicksand and I am sinking. I become terrified and every instinct tells me to move, but luckily I make myself stand still and breathe deeply. The sinking slows. I look around and see a young woman standing near the edge of the quicksand. Her dark hair is tied up in a bun, she is wearing a long, dark blue skirt, and a long sleeved, white blouse. I ask if she can help. She looks to the woods and beckons, a large elephant comes out and offers me his trunk, then pulls me free.

At this point I look around and notice that we are on an estate that looks both English and East Indian. It brought to mind the time when England had colonized India in the late 19th and early 20th centuries. There was an attempt at English gardening, which didn't work as well in the Indian climate. Women with red spots on their foreheads were working in the fields, trying to grow English crops. There was a large manor behind us, with an arched Verandah overlooking the gardens.

I was weak with relief and so grateful. The woman thanks the elephant and walks with me the short distance to the mansion. Just around the back of the building is a small, clear pond. There are several other ponds filled with large koi swimming. This one, however, is clear and she tells me to bathe in it, as I am still covered with mud. After I've washed - oh, how good that felt - she hands me a large, exquisitely soft white robe, like something from a fancy spa. I put it on, feeling cosseted.

We walk up the back steps and onto the sumptuous wrap-around porch. Lovely flowering vines climb around the wooden arches, and the view is gently rolling, almost like the English countryside - no wonder they wanted to colonize India! There are comfy lounge chairs with small tables beside them. She points me to an empty one, where I sink into just-right cushions. I ask if she is the spirit of this point, and she says yes.

"Being seriously ill is like being caught in quicksand," she explains. "Many people struggle and sink. It is difficult for them to know how much or when to fight, as well as when to let go. Dealing with illness often amounts to a dance between the two." She smiles at me. "And asking for help as you did is often a key component. After the illness is gone, rest is very important for renewal. Introspection and meditation or prayer help people to avoid further disease, and surrounding oneself with beauty and love helps to rebuild oneself. My medicine offers a quiet, beautiful, and comfortable place where people can recuperate." She motions to someone and a cup of hot tea materializes on the table beside me. She points toward the yard and I see again how very pretty everything is. Banks of flowers blaze bright in the sun, and the wood beyond looks invitingly cool. Somewhere out of sight there are roses. If I stayed here, I think, I could toddle out later and find the source of the glorious smell.

"This is a place to take in the beauty - literally," says the woman. "Your body needs to feel the beauty . . . You've come through the hard times? Now it's time to hang out and enjoy the view."

I sat there sipping tea and listening to the birds. I was so glad to be here and not to have died in the quicksand. I felt relief: my body was clean and warm, and the sun warmed my face. The tea was both spicy and sweet, and it filled my body with a liquidy relaxation.

I looked around and noticed other people sitting in chairs with robes and tea. There were attendants taking care of them. The air was slightly cool but not cold, and as well as roses, it smelled of sweet cut grass.

The woman returned, pulled up a chair, and sat down beside me. "When you have patients who have been sick," she says, "don't judge whether it is a 'serious' illness or a 'small' illness. Just know that they all need tending and rest in order to return to the fullness of their lives. This point, **Walking on the Verandah**, will help them with that. It offers a perspective of the vitality of life, something they can look forward to, while they sit comfortably on the verandah and are served."

I thanked her and returned to ordinary reality. Then I turned off the CD player and thought about "illness" or "disease." Disease (being not-at-ease) might manifest as a physical disorder, or it might manifest as emotional or mental disorders, and it might be an episode or it might be chronic, or it could be like I was, worrying about finances to the point of not being able to sleep -- and none of that mattered. I suddenly understood that this glorious point could be used for someone coming through *any* type of "dis-ease," which I did not have to evaluate. I just had to help. What a gift!

Section 3: Spring

There was a time in my life when I loved Spring as much as Autumn, and I do hope I get back to that love. Right now I am in that stage of a woman's life when heat is a constant threat — and while spring isn't hot, in the back of my mind lurks the knowledge that once it is spring, summer will come soon.

Aside from my personal issues with heat, spring initiates the rebirth of the cycle of life. All the Qi that had been pulled in to help life survive the Winter now moves up and out, in a movement that is forceful - even unstoppable: think of a daffodil shoot. It comes up fast, sometimes inches in a day, then *explodes* into bloom. (The shape and the speed of the bloom often make me think of popcorn.) The trees restore the Qi from the roots to the branches to produce a pink haze of buds, which fatten, then turn brilliant green. Often, if you watch a particular tree or bush, you will see the size of the leaves double in a single day. The birds fly back from their winter homes and begin creating new homes, making babies, and tormenting cats. Every day brings something new.

Spring is dramatic: not only does it move fast, but there is an aspect of surprise as life wakes up and declares itself. "HERE I AM!" shouts Spring. "I'm HE-E-ERE!"

While it may seem to us, that there is a wild craziness of popping flowers, scurrying critters and mating birds, Spring is actually orderly, like a parade. There is a plan, particular plants bloom in a particular order. Like the marching band following the dancers, who follow the football team.

The "translation of the translation" of the season's emotion is called "anger." Again, to our culture this word mis-states the essence of this season, as the essence of Spring movement is up and out, so its emotion is one of upwardness or uprightness -- not opposition. It is more a drive to see what needs to happen and make it happen, right now. Sometimes that means righting what is wrong. Think of Gandhi, advising non-violence as a way to throw off the colonial yoke, or the courageous people who fought for their freedom in our Revolutionary war. Think of the many folks who helped slaves escape, or those who helped others escape the Nazis. Our own civil rights movement and the campaign for women's suffrage also expresses the energy of spring. Expressing both the orderliness of which plants bud out first and the drama of the outward movement, the emotion of Spring is strategic, creative, and powerful. The true emotion of this season includes both the ability to see what needs to happen, then the foresight to make effective plans in a structured and creative way. Boom! Rain! Shoot! Bud! Daffodils! Done!

Rarely does this emotion explode for the benefit of the individual who feels it, rather it most often arises for the benefit of many. It's about the big picture, and I don't think we have a word in English that carries such a sense. "Passion" catches the force, but is so often purely personal. "Benevolence" is close, but a tad passive. Perhaps "passion for justice" speaks most closely to what is meant.

The organs or officials associated with Spring are the Gall Bladder and the Liver. As you notice the first plants who pop up in Spring, think of what they do: many have bitter leaves, like dandelions, arugula, and sorrel and are traditionally used to cleanse and detoxify the liver. The Chinese call the liver, the "general." A leader or general who is full of toxins (physically or emotionally) is one who lords his authority and belittles his subordinates. A clear-minded, right-spirited leader will guide and support the people with benevolence and creativity - the virtues of this season. Once the General (Liver) makes clear plans, the Gall Bladder, called the Decision Maker, comes in and makes all the little decisions to carry out the plans.

As we enjoy Spring, let our creativity flow. Start new things, spend time outside, and take in the deliciousness of the early plants who will help us live without toxicity and move out into the world with clarity and power.

Chapter 7: No Regrets - Gate of Hope (Liver 14)

Joni Mitchell's song "Big Yellow Taxi" has always aroused an emotion of regret in me. When I hear it, I remember all the good things in my life that have passed and wonder if I appreciated them enough. She talks about not realizing what we have until it is gone. Right on Joni. It's important to notice the losses of things we take for granted, like our environment -- she talks about the world being a paradise that we make into a parking lot. She reminds us that we wouldn't want a life or a planet cast in stone.

Daniel came to me about three years after his divorce. He was suffering from severe neck pain, which frequently produced headaches. He was missing a lot of work and was in danger of losing his job. He was angry over his divorce.

They had three children who were ages 15, 12 and 9. The youngest was a boy and the other two were girls.

"I wish I had never met her, all those years down the drain -- wasted," he said in the first interview. "Now, I have to work all the time to pay child support and alimony -- all for nothing." When he spoke, I could see tension in his shoulders and redness in his face. Such anger, it seemed fueled by something else, which I hadn't yet discovered.

"So, what do you do for a living?" I asked.

The redness in his face subsided and his eyes lit up, "I design video games." I could tell by his demeanor that he liked his job. His shoulders dropped down and he actually smiled.

"How long have you been doing that?"

"I started out in computer programming. I also studied graphic arts in college - digital that is. Then a friend showed me a listing for an entry level position at a large video game producer. They wanted someone with a programming and arts background and they said they'd train from there. I got the job and I have been there almost 20 years now. I am one of the main creators and I train new people."

"You must make a decent wage."

"Yea, a lot more than I ever thought I'd earn, and it is so much fun."

His tension and pain were gone as he talked about his work. "So," I continued, "when you say you work all the time to pay child support and alimony, and then you say you love your job, I am not understanding the problem. Do you not have enough left over for yourself?"

"Well, no, I have enough," his face reddened, his shoulders tensed up again, "I just hate having to pay money to that bitch after she stole all those years from me."

"How do you feel about your children?" I asked.

"I love them," he looked at me with a question in his eyes.

"Well, didn't they come from this union?"

"Yes, but . . ."

"So it wasn't wasted," I interrupted.

"I see what you mean, but my wife destroyed the family. She wanted out."

"That must have hurt," I said. I saw tears well up in his eyes. Ah, that's the missing piece. "You didn't want the marriage to end, did you?"

"No," he sniffed.

It came out over time that he and his wife had drifted apart, but he hadn't realized it, so it somewhat surprised him when his wife wanted the divorce. After treatment and coaching, he came to understand that his neck pain and headaches were how his body dealt with his unresolved hurt and resentment.

We talked over time about how his marriage wasn't a mistake, both of them were in love when they chose to marry, and they have beautiful children from that love. When he was able to let go of the hurt and resentment and express gratitude for the marriage, his neck pain and headaches became less frequent and finally went away. The last I heard, Daniel and his ex-wife have actually built a friendship, for the sake of their children.

Think about it: many Americans have an unstated assumption that everything should endure, so if something ends, ipso facto, there must be a problem.

When a marriage or a business ends, many of us shake our heads and wonder what went wrong. When someone dies, we may view death as "the enemy" that once more won the battle. When our children grow up and leave home, many people get depressed and we call it "empty nest syndrome." If we could ever get that nothing really ends, but rather comes and goes in cycles, from generation to generation, we could stop wasting precious time living in regret. What about celebrating the joy a marriage brought in its time? What about embracing the next phase of our lives when we have completed a job well-done in raising our children? When mother birds literally kick the baby birds out of the nest, we don't suggest antidepressants. I am not suggesting that there aren't real feelings we experience with these changes, a grieving process. What I am talking about is living in regret long after the grieving period. Grieving is a necessary process, but defining one's life by the "what if's" only creates suffering and dis-"ease".

When a gourmet meal is finished, do we mourn its end? Do we declare that because it is over, we should never have sat down to eat? Just because something has run its course doesn't mean it was a mistake. Knowing that, we can carry with us the gifts that all our various experiences have brought us - if we take the time to remember and express gratitude for them. It is when we experience gratitude, we can have hope to move forward into the world.

We never really lose *anything*. We carry within our bodies the experiences that we have from our whole lives. Details of the memory may change as we who have the memories grow and learn. For example, some memories of my mother have morphed since I came to understand more about the middle years of life. The essence of having been mothered by her remains, however. No one and nothing can take those experiences from me. I can remember, and in that remembering, feel once again the joy and happiness those experiences brought. In our consumerist culture, striving for more and more possessions, it is easy to forget that we already have it all.

Healing, then, whether by needles or a shamanic session, does not mean giving people something they don't already have; it is reminding them what they have, not least, their own divine ability to heal themselves. I am reminded of another song by the group *America*, where the lyrics remind us that we already have everything we need, as the Tin-man in the *Wizard of Oz* already exhibited signs of having a heart before the Wizard supposedly gave it to him. The brainwashing of Modern Western culture is all about acquiring and striving, without reflection and gratitude. This blindness is a source of tremendous dis-ease, and stuck-ness.

Deep grief, depression, or psychosis can rob a person of good memories, if only by making those memories seem unreal and unreliable. I emphatically do not wish to say that emotional suffering is chosen or imaginary. At the same time, for many of us, there is an element of choice. In my experience if I spend my time remembering my losses, without remembering my joys, it would be understandable to become hopeless or to give up. It seems to me, good medicine might be coaching people to recall the gifts within their losses, as I did with Daniel, and to notice if they had not lived, loved, and lost, they would be void of many gifts.

Hope

Hope is the thing with feathers
That perches in the soul,
And sings the tune--without the words,
And never stops at all. (1)

The choice is to focus on the loss and give away hope, or to focus on the gifts allowing the bird of hope to perch in our soul, and never stop at all.

(1) *The Poems of Emily Dickinson* Edited by R. W. Franklin (Harvard University Press, 1999).

Gate of Hope - The journey

This pair of points is located on the rib cage in a little notch several inches below the nipples. I enter the point on my ribs and feelmyself falling through space, falling, falling, falling . . I land softly. It is night and the grass is soft. Overhead, the stars look like a trillion diamonds and there are fireflies flitting about. I also notice a garden gate with vines entwined around the fence. I am very tired, so I lie down and fall asleep on the grass, till I am awakened suddenly by a young woman with long platinum hair, which is flowing in the early morning breeze. She is pulling me to my feet. As I stand up, I notice she has on a soft sheer, peach colored dress, that is also blowing in the breeze.

"Hurry up and wake," she says. "I'm Hope, and this is my gate. You don't want to miss this."

I stand up and brush the dew from my clothes. I am not only damp, but a trifle chilly. Hope holds my arm firmly and I feel steady. We stand in silence watching the gate. Just when I start to think this is crazy, a million birds begin chirping, almost like a symphony. And as the first rays of sunlight hit the intricately woven designs of the metallic gate, it begins to show gold. Suddenly I am aware that I am more than chilly, and that the sunlight is exquisitely warm as it hits my legs. As the sun rises higher and higher, the entire gate turns to gold, inset with beautiful gems. It is sparkling, magnificent.

"Whoa," I gasp.

Hope smiles and looks at me, her eyes a light crystalline green, shining with tears. "Every morning the sun rises. Some days you can't see it because of clouds, but you know it is there. Night does not last forever! In the same way, every Spring the Winter recedes, bringing back lush grass and new seedlings."

She leads me through the golden, jeweled gate to a bench in the garden. I notice morning glories popping open on the fence. A bluebird lands on the bench beside us and Hope pulls some bird seed out of a pouch and tosses it on the ground. Many birds flutter to the ground and begin to eat. I look out into this amazing garden to see masses of daffodils, tulips, and irises. Outside of the fence there's a family of deer - a doe, a buck, and two fawns. They don't seem to be afraid of us.

"Use this point," says Hope, "to help your patients know that whatever they are experiencing as painful, dark, or hopeless will end. The Sun will rise. The Spring will come. Life will start again, over and over again. That is what hope is all about. Having hope doesn't mean that you will never experience difficult or challenging times -- it means that it won't last. Every morning is an opportunity to start again, and every evening is the opportunity to let go of the struggle, even if only for the moment."

I am so filled with the beauty of this place and of Hope, the spirit of the point that I don't want to leave. Hope smiles. "Take the beauty with you." She hugs me and I come back.

When my daughters grew up and left home, I entertained the "empty nest syndrome" for a couple of weeks. Then I bought some paint and painted my youngest daughter's room and made it into a guest/sewing room. These days, when my daughters come home to visit, I find that a new relationship with them has been arising. They are my best friends, my strongest advocates, and my confidantes. I delight in their presence. I have never loved anyone in any situation as much as I love them. They dazzle and amaze me. If they had never grown up or left, I could not know them this way.

Chapter 8: The Big Picture: Sun and Moon (Gall Bladder 24)

I turned 23 during the honeymoon of my first marriage. Then eleven moths later, I gave birth to my first daughter. Surprise! I was in school, studying Art, and we had planned for me to finish school before having children. I was not a happy camper to be pregnant so soon. I had an IUD and had thought I was safe. Now the IUD had to come out, a procedure with an 80% chance of causing miscarriage. As the weeks of that danger passed, it was clear that God really wanted me to have this baby.

I spent the whole pregnancy pissed off at God. I was rebellious, meaning I didn't give up *anything* for this unplanned baby. I went to painting classes, spending hours in rooms filled with heavy turpentine fumes. The teacher suggested I might not want to be there, but I refused to leave. People told me that my anger would shift when I felt the baby move, but that didn't happen (because I didn't let it). We both were not happy about having a baby, in fact, we even looked into putting the baby up for adoption, we felt so trapped. As I think back on it, if either of us could have been positive about the situation, I think the other would have come around, but as it was, we were both metaphorically shaking our fists at God.

Then, to top it all off, the baby was in a breech position, all poised to deliver fanny-first, so that a vaginal delivery posed a problem. I tried everything I could think of to get her to turn, and the doctor did painful manipulations, but nothing worked. I even spent hours lying on an inclined board with my head down and feet up to try to turn her. It was as if this baby were showing me she was just as rebellious as I was. (Too bad I didn't know anything about acupuncture, as there is a point that will turn breech babies.) I called all over trying to find someone who would deliver a breech baby vaginally, to no avail. So, the weary weeks passed until Saturday morning, June 26, 1982. When I woke up around 7:00 am, my husband asked me what I wanted to do that day, but not even 10 seconds later I felt my first contraction. I knew what we were going to do that day -- a Caesarean section.

By the time we got to the hospital, I was having contractions 2 to 3 minutes apart. Since we knew I was going to have a Caesarean, the doctor skipped the pelvic exam. Instead, they monitored contractions while they prepared me for surgery. I felt completely out of control, as if I were hurtling down some huge water slide to doom.

I was awake during the surgery, numb and nauseated from spinal anesthesia. I was also unable to see what was happening because there was a curtain hung across my waist. I felt disembodied tugging and pulling, then I heard a cry. They brought her around for me to see. Until that moment, I was only focused on my own discomfort.

Nothing in my life had prepared me for that moment when I first looked into her eyes. If any of my friends had tried to tell me about "bonding," I would have laughed them off. Yet there it was: the moment I looked into her eyes, I was in complete and total love. I had never experienced anything like it before. One moment I was indifferent and the next moment I would have killed to protect this baby. All these years later, I am still at a loss of words to describe this instantaneous transformation. They say a birth is a miracle, and while that may very well be true, from my experience becoming a mother is also a miracle.

This daughter (who I will call Bethany) turned out to be a difficult baby. For the first four months, she was so colicky and fussy that she had to be jiggled and walked all day long. Otherwise, she'd scream. I was alone in the house, so when I left her to shower or cook, she would scream the whole time, whether I was gone 15 minutes or 2 hours. When someone gave me a baby swing, I thought I had died and gone to heaven. Wow! I could wind it up and have 15 minutes of silence! Even after the colic passed, I would spend hours holding her, nursing and loving her. I quit school and became a stay-at-home mom.

Breast pumps in those days were inadequate, and I didn't want her to have formula.

Bethany was a difficult toddler as well. I think she is an old soul who was frustrated at being in the body of a toddler when she had so many things to do. She was an amazing teenager - full of creativity, vision, laughter, and wisdom. In spite of an ADD diagnosis, she graduated from high school on the honor roll without medication. She was in the drama club; she spent hours after school in the high school dark room developing black and white photos, and she was a mainstay of the literary magazine.

Both my daughters are now my best friends. I trust them and know they want the best for me, as I do for them.

I am so grateful to God that the circumstances were just right for me to have my first daughter. If I hadn't been in that fundamentalist church, I would likely have had an abortion and missed one of the greatest gifts in my life. Don't mistake me for an anti-abortionist, though: I believe the choice belongs to the mother, and that such a choice is so heart-wrenching that no one should be harassed by some outsider who has no stake in the outcome.

Bethany has always been an activist. She has marched for gay rights, women's rights, animal rights, minority rights, and probably other rights I'm not aware of. I am very proud of the work she does. She recently finished her master's degree in Education and secured a job at a last-chance High School where she is writing a new curriculum for history and social studies as well as teaching the subjects.

In 2012 she got married in New York State. They held the wedding at a Buddhist Temple/retreat center, and every detail of the wedding, from our arrival on Friday to our leaving after Sunday brunch, spoke of the couple's incredible love, creativity, and attention to detail. They joined a flower CSA (Community Supported Agriculture program) and got beautiful flowers by the bucket. After arrival, all the guests and family pitched in to help create the event. Some helped with food, while others kept an eye on the children who were playing around the grounds. Some arranged flowers, while others helped assemble place settings. There was a blue grass band that came on the wedding night for wild dancing and fun, and the whole event was brilliant -- an instant village. By the time we left on Sunday, it felt as if the families were joined, not simply the two people.

In a later chapter I will tell a story about my younger daughter (who I will call Noel) and dandelions. Both daughters are unique in their gifts, thinking about them fills my heart.

Sun and Moon - the journey

In this journey, after turning on the CD player, I start by walking my fingers up the ribcage from the bottom towards the armpit. When I reach the seventh intercostal space I drop into the point, which feels to the finger like an inviting little nook, a place where the finger "wants to stay. Yet once I'm in the nook, I find myself floating in deep space. I see Earth, the sun, the moon and several other planets of this solar system, glowing against the star-filled universe.

"When you are here, things are in perspective, aren't they?" A voice next to me makes me jump.

I look over to where the voice is coming from and I see -- I kid you not -- the Energizer Bunny. "Oh, no! You are *not* the spirit of this point, are you?"

The bunny starts laughing. "Why not?" He bangs his little drum and does somersaults, huge somersaults, in the no-gravity of space. I find I am laughing as well.

"So, Bunny, what is the medicine of this point?"

"Follow me," says the bunny, and suddenly it is as though we are swimming through space till we reach the moon. We sit down next to the flagpole left by the moon walkers of 1969. "You humans think you're so much in control, don't you?" he asks rhetorically. "So, the decisions you make in your small lives often lack the perspective of the big picture. You didn't have the big picture when you were pregnant with your first daughter. If you had finished art school and become an art teacher as you planned, you would not have helped the many, many people you have reached as an acupuncturist.

"For your patients," he continued, "use this point when they have lost perspective and can't see the big picture. This point helps them draw a bigger circle. Sun and Moon can be seen in opposition to each other. Yet if you had only day and no night, all the plants would die. And if you had no day and only night, all the plants would still die. Day and night are never in opposition - they are only relatively opposite. The bigger picture places them as two parts of a whole cycle of 24 hours."

The silence on the moon is deep, profound and all encompassing. I think I would like to stay here.

"Silence is part of the big picture," Bunny says. "However, if all you had was silence, you'd miss out on all the rest life has to offer. Remind your patients to enjoy the whole enchilada."

I laugh at this reference. We "swim" back to where I started and I return to myself.

After turning off the CD player I begin to think about this message. There were some very horrible things that happened in the middle after my first divorce and where we are now. When I talk about my daughters, it may seem like I am "whitewashing" it. There are plenty of areas that still need love, forgiveness and healing, always for all of us. Just remember: Love *is* the big picture.

Chapter 9: Pets - Foot above Tears (Gall Bladder 42)

The dilemma people face with pets is that, most often, we outlive them. I have heard people say that they avoid owning pets because they can't handle the pain of their dying. So the question is: How can we open our hearts to these valuable beings, even knowing we must lose them?

When I was a teenager, my mother had a cat named Misty, who was the smartest cat I have ever met. She was Siamese, though not pedigreed, and full of "hiss and vinegar." When I was 11, we lived on a Navy Base where yards were not fenced. Many residents let their dogs run free, so the dogs would come around and poop in other peoples' yards. Misty not only disapproved, but she took effective action: she would sit in the rafters of our carport and guard her turf. She drew a clear boundary around our house, and whenever some hapless dog would wander inside her invisible line, she would leap down and chase the offender. Many a time she would actually jump on their backs, claws inserted, and *ride* them out of the yard, yipping all the way. It was quite a sight! (I wouldn't have believed if I hadn't seen it with my own eyes.) Within a few months of our arrival, all the dogs in the neighborhood knew Misty's boundaries and stayed away.

Misty was only with us for six years, but she left an amazing imprint in that time. We got her in Florida, moved on to the Navy Base, got transferred to Maryland, lived in two different places in Maryland, and then moved back to Florida. (Dad was a career Navy man.)

Once back in Florida, we lived out in the "boonies," in a town south of Jacksonville called Middleburg. My parents rented a double-wide trailer on several acres that backed up to woods all around, and we had ducks, geese, chickens, and quail. The place came with a large old black labrador named Cinder, who had obviously been around cats in her days. Misty and Cinder tolerated each other, and things were good until one day Misty disappeared. We spent weeks combing the woods, calling and calling. At first Mom thought she'd been stolen, as she was a stunningly beautiful Siamese, but we gave up that theory on the grounds that Misty was so bad-mannered with strangers that any thief would surely let her go. We finally decided that she must have been bitten by a rattlesnake or water moccasin, perhaps while trying to ride it out of her invisible kingdom.

Mom was heartbroken. She *loved* that cat, and to this day, almost 40 years later, she refuses to get attached to an animal. My dad has had several dogs and cats through the years, whom my mom treats with disdain (not abusive), calling them names like "ugly" or "hateful." My daughters think she is horrible (in this instance), but I know this behavior comes from a wound that never healed. She doesn't hate animals: rather, she loves them so much that she dares not let herself care.

Pets have much to teach us, because unlike people, pets have no capacity to judge. They are present to their senses and they can sense danger, fear, acceptance, and love. Whatever we emit, they reflect back to us.

Thinking of Mom and Misty, I realize people who seem "mean" or "hateful" are not horrible people. They are often people whose hearts are so wounded that they're terrified to let anyone in. Really, rather than hating, they love so deeply they dare not open their wounded hearts. If we hold this possibility, how will it change our interactions with the hurtful, hurting people whom we meet?

Foot above tears - the journey

I sit down on my floor and pick up my drum. As I enter the journey state, I go to the top of my foot where the fourth and fifth ("little") toe bones meet, then sink into the point. I am slipping down a tunnel as if I were sliding down a slide. The trip speed is very fast, and it seems to go on forever. As I finally thud to a halt, my vision clears and I find myself in a trackless swamp. I look around hoping to find the spirit of the point, or at least a path, but there's nothing and no one to see, just swamp - until I hear weeping and I follow the sound. I am picking my way through wet, muddy plants, and because I have lived in Florida, I walk noisily, keeping a lookout for snakes. I walk past a tree, and come upon a small man sitting with his back against the tree, knees pulled up. He is hugging his legs with his arms and his face is down on his knees. He is weeping - a loud wailing sound.

"Are you okay?" I ask. He looks up with tears glistening in his bushy beard, which is brown flecked with grey. He jumps up, startling me, and I see he is about half my height, like one of Snow White's dwarf friends. His brown trousers have suspenders over a light blue shirt. He is grinning now, and if his beard were not still wet, I would never have known he was crying a moment before. He beckons me to follow, and I do. He must have an understanding with the snakes, as he moves at a rapid clip. I still don't see any path, but clearly, he does. We're going straight out of the swamp and into a dense and shaggy forest.

In the forest, rays of sunlight find their way through holes in a low canopy, moving around on a forest floor that is covered with decaying leaves and fallen branches. The forest smells earthy and close, redolent of soil and leaves - much like the smell of patchouli. The little man stops in front of a "father of trees", one that towers over the rest of the trees. There are boards nailed onto its trunk forming a ladder that goes all the way to the crown. He starts climbing and motions for me to follow, and I do. As we move higher and higher, I am sweating with exertion, and my heart is pounding to the distant rhythm of the drum. The climb seems to go on forever -- a hot and sweaty forever - till finally we push through the canopy onto a platform, where a cool, heavenly breeze hits my sweaty face. As my breath slows I can take in the tops of the trees in all directions. They too, seem to go on forever from distant mountains looming in one direction, to the ocean pounding the shore in the other. The sea breeze smells salty and refreshing.

The dwarf's face no longer shows that he's been crying. He is smiling broadly at me. "Are you the spirit of this point?" I ask him.

Nodding, he says, "yes."

"Can you tell me about your wisdom/medicine?"

"I just did," he says. "I am the point that leads you out of the tearful swamp of stagnation and frustration, through the forest of confusion, and up above the forest to where you can see clearly. When you offer this point to your patients, they will see clearly and rise above their tears."

I can suddenly hear the words to a famous song by Johnny Nash, about seeing clearly when the rain is gone. I start to sing it — I can't help it.

The dwarf laughs. "If you know that song, you know this point."

We climb down and I return to ordinary reality. Putting my drum down, I pick up my laptop to write down this story.

As I think more about my mother and her hurt-based disdain for pets, I see her spirit stuck in the swamp of stagnation, crying for the cat she loved and lost. In general she is a generous person, who I know loves me, I just think her pain over this cat caused her to be stuck when it comes to animals. How can I offer her the possibility of rising above her tears so she can reopen her heart? If I were her acupuncturist, I would treat this point (among others). However, it isn't a great idea to treat family members. So my challenge will be to *become* the energy of this point. I must find a way to *be* "Foot Above Tears" for my mother.

Section 4: Summer

When I was a young mom, I lived in Southern California and Summer was fun fun fun! My kids would be home from school and on many weekends we went camping. Since the climate is dry there, bugs and mosquitoes were rare and camping was idyllic. We'd spend days on the beach digging in the sand and making sand castles. Then in the evenings we'd sit up late around the campfire, singing and telling stories and toasting marshmallows.

Summer is the time when all trees and plants are at their peak. The buds have become leaves, the flowers are thriving, and a cascade of delicious food comes ripe, starting with strawberries. Summer is associated with maturity.

I personally find the split personality of this season both amusing and profound. The power and smoothness of maturity combined with eagerness to play suggests to me what the mature person knows: too much seriousness is bad for you. Love is associated with Summer, too, in a different sense than the love of spring. In the spring, there's a lot of mating and production of young, yet sexuality is more associated with the summer. My understanding is that the sexuality of spring is like the beginning of a relationship, when everything is hot, heavy, and delirious, while the sexuality of summer connotes a more mature, relaxed, and heart-centered kind of love.

The organs (or officials) of summer are the the Heart, the Pericardium, the Small Intestines and the Three Heater. (The three what? you may ask . . . Relax. We'll get there.) The Heart is like a campfire, people are drawn to it --even mesmerized by it. The Heart draws people together, which makes sense because it also plays the role of the Emperor. It's the "Supreme Controller," holding up a ceremonial bowl to catch and facilitate the will of heaven. The Pericardium, anatomically, is the sack around the Heart. As the official, it is the ambassador to the Heart. It speaks for the Heart and protects the Heart by means of its gates, which open and close either to let people into to the inner sanctuary (of the Heart) or to keep people out who would injure the Heart. The Small Intestines sorts the pure from the impure, a different form of service to the Heart and the will of heaven, while the Three Heater represents the "the host with the most." Physically, this official is not an organ; it is more like an organ system. It functions to make sure that all the organs and parts of the body stay at the "right" temperature to do their work well. In the psychological/social realm, the Three Heater makes sure that everyone at a party is happy and taken care of, as the Heart would want. In fact, all three officials -- Pericardium, Small Intestines and Three Heater -- are servants of the Heart, because Summer is all about the Heart. A person with true maturity understands matters of the Heart and knows how to hold others in love, even difficult people.

When I think of these officials, I sometimes think of preparing a candlelit dinner for my beloved. My Heart wants to deeply connect with the Heart of my dear one. Since this is summer and not spring, my beloved and I have weathered some time together, so although sometimes the "feeling" of love is absent, the _choice_ of love is always present. My Pericardium is there to protect my heart, - so instead of planning a surprise and risking disappointment when the beloved does not come, my Pericardium reminds me to tell my beloved that I am preparing a special dinner. My Small Intestine, the Sorter of the Pure from Impure, chooses the menu, (again in service to my Heart), so I will fix what my beloved likes, not just what I like. Once we begin to eat, my Three Heater, will be assessing the emotional temperature of the dinner: is my beloved enjoying the food, the drink, the conversation? Are we in harmony?

Metaphorically, this scene describes a mature relationship, one in which I know the flaws of my beloved, and my beloved knows mine. We've been through the phase of infatuation and lust, and have chosen to accept and love each other exactly as we truly are, for better and for worse. Love at this point is no longer a feeling that comes and goes, but rather a deep appreciation of the gifts and blessings we are to each other -- together with an understanding that life may take us away from each other at times, and that therefore we must make time to stoke the fires of love, and know that the other is doing the same. This is joy.

The emotion of summer (you know the drill: it's a translation of the translation) is joy. Once again, joy is a word we understand differently in our modern culture than did the ancient Chinese. In Western culture joy is often confused with happiness. In Chinese thought, happiness is more of a choice, a mood that we can control. Joy is much deeper. In a state of joy, we accept all that is and are willing to see whatever life brings as a blessing, whether or not it was part of our plan. The plan arose from the spring, and has the qualities of spring: sharp vision and directed action. Summer is more about the way the plan manifests, affected as it is by chance events. Perhaps the timing and amount of rain were perfect, and perhaps they were not. Whatever happened, in summer the harvest matures and we should greet it with love and acceptance.

Likewise, in dealing with people outside our intimate circle, summer reminds us to practice the love and inclusiveness that community needs, framing each person in acceptance. Acceptance is effectively absolute: <u>however</u> the person matured - "autistic," crabby, touchy, prone to fish all the cashews out of the trail mix - there they are, part of the community. Maturity helps us live with people as they are - and ourselves as well, imperfect as we also are.

On a larger scale, summer is all about the communication and relationships important in all parts of our lives - our families, friends, children, grandchildren, and colleagues. It is no accident that summer is the time when families tend to rejoin, meeting for vacation to renew and enjoy the love of family and to bring on new children and friends. Our maturity is about basking in the warmth of those things that serve our hearts.

The bottom line: our wise hearts know that the materialistic busy-ness with which we fill our lives is not what's important. What truly matters is the connection with our many beloveds. To know and act upon our love is the wisdom of summer.

Chapter 10: The Lesson of a Living/Dying Patient: Palace of Weariness (Pericardium 8)

When I first moved to Maryland, I bought an existing Acupuncture practice from an established practitioner. Buying a practice can be tricky because, in brute fact, the assets of the practice are the patients - who cannot, of course, be truly bought or sold. They are free to stay or go. So my task was to build rapport with the patients before their old practitioner left. Otherwise, all I would have purchased was a list of names.

The departing practitioner handled her task with care and generosity, introducing me personally to each of her patients. She also spent time coaching me about each of them in private, to help me serve them well - which brings me to Peggy. Peggy had been a patient for several years and had a very serious heart condition called myocarditis. Patients who get this diagnosis usually die soon thereafter, so at the time I met Peggy, we all "knew" she had a limited time to live.

The departing practitioner said to me, "Peggy's dying; she's just living in denial." I believe if the departing practitioner hadn't been pregnant and focused on her new life, she may have looked at Peggy differently.

This statement landed on me like a cast iron frying pan upside the head, especially after I fully took over the practice and looked at Peggy's records, for It was clear that Peggy's treatment plan was based on that pronouncement - "dying." Points had been chosen not to enhance or balance her constitution, but simply to lessen her symptoms. It was a mechanical, repetitive approach to treatment, aimed at "getting her through" or something like that. When I talked with Peggy, however, I found she had a lot to live for. She had a 16-year-old daughter whom she wanted to see graduate from high school; she loved her job; she loved to travel; and she sang in a choir in Washington, DC. Her life was full. She knew her time was limited. At the same time, she wanted to get every ounce of joy from the time she had left. So I planned treatments that would help her do that.

About five years into treatment with me, Peggy had a stroke and lost her ability to swallow. (At that point her daughter had not only graduated from high school, but also was a student at NYU.) As well as a loving daughter, Peggy had many, many friends who called me to come treat her in the hospital. Now, I am sure the reader may not understand the political issues around an Acupuncturist treating a patient in an Allopathic system like a western hospital, but suffice it to say it is not allowed. Even if I held a license to practice in Washington, D.C., where the hospital was, it would not have been allowed. I didn't think I'd be able to do anything for Peggy except visit. However, her friends whisked me into the room and commanded me to treat her, while they stood guard outside the door and told the nurses that Peggy was with her "spiritual counselor." And so she was, in fact.

Peggy was released from the hospital with a feeding tube in her stomach, a situation that often leads to hospice - but not for Peggy. To show you the power of her will, within a week she had found and was seeing a biofeedback therapist, who helped her regain her ability to swallow in just a few months. Is this the way of someone in denial? No. Here was someone with a very strong will to live each moment to the fullest. She and her daughter even made one more trip to Europe, post-stroke.

In the year 2000, I took my daughter to England as a high school graduation gift, and while we were away, Peggy took a turn for the worst; the only way she might survive would be with a heart transplant. Meanwhile, she lay in the hospital waiting for one, in such bad shape that the medical team induced a coma. Something went wrong, however, and her brain function ceased. Her daughter was offered the hardest of choices, to shut down the machines. Peggy died while I was gone.

At Peggy's funeral, the church was packed. I had to sit in the balcony, as every single seat was taken. One after another, dozens of friends, co-workers, and family got up to share the deep ways that Peggy had touched them. Her daughter, Caitlin, read a poem she had written about her mom. We all wept.

After the service, I went up to Caitlin, whom I had never met before, and told her I was her mom's acupuncturist. Caitlin threw her arms around me and said, "My mom loved you so much."

Peggy reinforced for me an essential lesson from my training: I don't get to decide who is dying and who is not. I don't get to decide how and where a patient uses their Qi. I don't get to decide what is important in a patient's life. My job is to support my patients to live their choices to the fullest.

I could have said, "Peggy, you need to slow down and conserve your energy. Your body is exhausted and your heart is shutting down. As it is, when I treat you, you turn around and burn up the energy to maintain your busy lifestyle."

Sounds good, right? It sounds reasonable, like straight talk from one who knows to the patient. But would it have helped Peggy live longer? I doubt it. She might have died sooner if she gave in to her exhaustion. At one point she was interviewed at a grand rounds for cardiologists because she was the only person in the United States who had lived more than 5 years with myocarditis. Not only that: by the time she died, Peggy had lived close to 15 years with the illness. In those years she traveled to Europe several times; she traveled to South America; she sang in her choir in the National Cathedral; she raised a brilliant and self-sufficient daughter; and she touched and inspired many, many people. If that's denial, I'm all for it!!!

Palace of Weariness - the journey

This point is located on the palm of the hand where the life line intersects with the heart line, between the middle finger and the ring finger. This is usually where artists depict the nails in Jesus' hands. I turn on the CD. In the journey, I am walking on a dirt road, tired and thirsty, when in the distance I see a beautiful palace. It looks like something out of Disney, but real, made of glass and adorned with jewels and crystals. As the sun hits it, the sparkle can be seen for miles. I think, well, I might as well go there, and trudge on.

I am not sure why I feel so tired and heavy, but in this journey that is what I feel. My animal guide also seems to be tired, heavy and thirsty. It feels like hours before we approach the palace. Indeed, we both collapse near the door, unable to muster up the last few steps.

To our shock, a holy and royal person bursts out of the palace with his aides and they pick us up and carry us into the palace.

Just inside the door is a sparkling fountain, from which the holy man scoops water into a silver cup and brings it to me, holding it to my lips. The water is cool and slightly effervescent and as I drink, I feel life flowing through my body. This must be the water of life, I think. The holy man does the same for my animal guide, and within moments we are both lively and awake. I ask the man if he is the spirit of this point, and he says, Yes, that he is the Emperor of this palace, The Palace of Weariness. Why would an Emperor be taking personal care of strangers? I ask. He says simply, "That is the way of the Divine." His eyes sparkle, filled with Shen (Chinese for spirit.) Then he goes on to tell me that we are not strangers. He knows us and was expecting us. He offers us a tour of the palace.

One room is carpeted with soft, lush grass, and people are lying in the grass looking up at the sky through the glass ceiling. Another room has places for people to meditate. Yet another room is like a bedroom; a frail person is lying on a comfortable bed, a beautiful wolf reclining next to her. The holy man turns to me and says, "Some people need to stay in the Palace for the remainder of their lives."

"When you use this point," the Emperor tells me once we are back at the fountain, "know that weariness comes in many levels. Some people are so tired they think they cannot go on, yet a little water restores them to full vitality. Others are on their last threads of life and need to stay here. Take these people to my palace every time you treat them. Other types of weariness are caused by over busyness - not taking time to dream, imagine, or meditate. In such a case, you may need to use the point several times, to nudge them into taking time to restore themselves."

I say goodbye to the Emperor, who gives me a vigorous hug and several flasks filled with water of life. I know his presence will always be with me. My guide and I walk back down the road, completely recovered. Then I return to ordinary reality and turn off the CD player.

My dear patient, Peggy, lived in the Palace of Weariness. When she walked in, sometimes I could barely feel her pulses. (In Chinese medicine there are twelve pulses -- six on each wrist, one for each official). Then I would treat the Palace, after which I could feel faint weak pulses, pulses like a whisper. They were better than when she arrived, yet it was clear there wasn't much life energy to be called up. Given her frailty then, what she did with that little bit of Qi was amazing. She touched hundreds of people with her light. I carry a piece of her light in my soul, and whenever I treat someone on the Palace of Weariness, I believe she is there helping me.

Chapter 11: My Dad - Nourishing the Old (Small Intestine 6)

I was the first born in my family, arriving when my father was 24 years old and my mother 18. I have already shared with you the hardships my mother faced growing up, and suffice it to say, at 18 she wasn't ready to be a mother. She still had a lot of growing up to do herself.

My father was delighted to have a darling little girl, and we became best buds. I remember many fun times with him when I was tiny. I was born in Lynn, Massachusetts, and I remember playing outside in the snow with my dad. He really liked throwing snowballs! I used to accompany him down in the dark basement as he shoveled coal into the furnace to heat our home. When we moved to Texas, I remember running into the house (something for which my mom yelled at me) and slipping on the linoleum; my mom yelled at me, but my dad would pick me up and comfort me. And then there was our kiddie pool outside. My dad would be right there in the water with my brother and me, splashing away. I remember having a stomach flu, when my mom was in the hospital giving birth to my sister, and my dad was right there holding the bucket.

When I was eight, during the Vietnam war, my father was transferred from shore duty to sea duty — a shocking change to us all. We had to move from Texas to Florida, and what was worse, on sea duty Daddy would be gone for six months at a time — home for one month, gone for eleven months, home for a month, and so on for four years. When he would come home, it seemed we'd hardly get reacquainted before he was gone. Six months is a long time to a small child, let alone eleven months. By the time Daddy got back to shore duty, I was 12.

After the years of separation, things were never quite the same for my Daddy and me. I was in puberty and hormonal. I was argumentative and rebellious. My mother was frustrated with me, so my father decided it was his responsibility to "straighten me out," which only made me buck harder. We were so much at odds that I remember telling him I hated his guts, which was not the kind of language I was allowed to use in our home. So of course, it was natural that my sister, who was seven years my junior, took the role of daddy's darling, while I played the rebellious, teenage monster. Oh, where was the nice daddy who'd held the bucket, threw snowballs, splashed in the pool? I still find myself teary when I think about those early teen years.

Happily, I managed to make something shift as I neared the big 16, because I still wanted a relationship with my dad, who was back on sea duty, but would to be home for my birthday itself. So, when my mom asked me what I wanted for my 16th birthday, I told her I wanted to go on my first date — and I wanted that date to be with my dad. She smiled. Later, she told me that when she shared my request with my Dad, he cried.

Sweet Sixteen: I got dressed up in a store-bought, blue dress, and my dad bought me a corsage. We went to my favorite restaurant, which was a seafood restaurant, even though my dad hates fish (born and raised in Boston and hates fish - go figure!). After dinner, he took me to the Chief's club on the Navy Base to go dancing. It was one of the sweetest nights of my life. My friends thought I was nuts, as it wasn't cool to like one's parents in the '70s. I will never forget how proud he was of me that night.

That beautiful evening reopened the shut door between us in a remarkable way. For example, my high school had created a place on campus where students could smoke, but then one fall they decided to crack down and abolished the smoking area, as well as other "unfair" rules. Well! My friends and I were all smokers. My parents were fine with it; they wished I wouldn't, I suppose, but preferred me to smoke openly at home rather than sneak around. (My smoking friends thought I was really lucky.) So what business did the school have messing in this issue? Indignant, we decided to stage a protest walkout one morning in October. We posted big signs all over the school during the week before — which the school kept ripping down, of course, but we persisted, reposting signs almost as fast as they could tear them down. The morning of the walkout, my dad drove me to school and I told him what we were doing and why. I was amazed at his reaction: he told me to be careful, but to stand up for what I believed in. Wow! My dad was taking me seriously.

About an hour later came the moment of confrontation: I was one of some hundred students standing on the school parking lot waving signs and chanting for our "rights," while the principal, the vice principal, and a guidance counselor faced us down. Then, one student who really didn't get the idea of peaceful protest threw an egg at the school. The vice principal ran at him and most of the 100 students panicked and fled. I laughed about it later - as though one middle-aged guy could catch 100 students. I shook my head and went to class.

Inevitably, the protest had made me late to class and my teacher now said the tardy was unexcused and that she would have to call my parents. What could I do? I gave her my dad's work number and awaited events. Now, this particular teacher had once before "caught" me smoking, so she seized the opportunity to not only tell my dad about the walkout, but also that his daughter *smoked*. Well, that bomb was a dud, and so was the walkout. He'd known about them both! My dad told the teacher that he'd told me to stand up for my beliefs. Later, the teacher reported to me how impressed she was with the honest communication I had with my father. It hadn't occurred to her that he might know what I was up to -- that a father and daughter could actually be honest with each other. I was really proud of us!

My dad is now in his 80s and hard of hearing because he worked on jet planes for so many years. When I visit, it is difficult to have a conversation, yet, we manage, because he is still my dad, my bud with the bucket, _and_ my first date, _and_ the man no other man in this world could ever live up to. If you are reading this, I love you, Daddy!

Nourishing the Old - the journey

On the floor comfortable on the pillows, I begin to drum and find myself walking through a farmers' market. The place is a feast for the senses - there are so many different goods on offer: fruits, vegetables, crafts, home baked goods, eggs, cheese, and meats. I am moving from color to color, smell to smell: entranced by berry smells, honey . . . fresh baked bread . . . oh yum, coffee . . . when an elderly man approaches me. I ask if he is the spirit of the point and he nods. I slip my hand into his bent elbow and we stroll slowly through the market.

"What do you think your father would like?" he asks me.

I think about it, knowing this conversation isn't really about physical nourishment.

"When my Nana was alive and I lived 3000 miles away, I sent her a letter every week for years. My mom said those letters meant the world to her. Perhaps I could do something like that for my dad?"

"Your dad loves the letters you send him. He always has. Since he is deaf and it is hard to talk with him, letters seems like a choice that would serve him," he says, his eyes twinkling. "And remember," he adds, "that this point, Nourishing the Old, is on the Small Intestine meridian, which separates the pure from the impure. Another way to say it is that the point helps a person separate what will serve from what will not. Nourish your father with what will serve him."

"So, is that the medicine of this point?"

"Look around - this market is much like the world as a whole! There is so much to choose from -- too much, really. You can't give all that is available to an older person - any person - and you can't nourish the wisdom of the elders in yourself with everything that is available. You must make choices. Even the young people in this world, who are used to feeding their senses with anything that comes along, must learn to make choices -- you chose to experience your first date with your father. This decision served to nourish not only your father, but yourself and the father you hold inside yourself. Use this point for anyone who needs help in nourishing their wisdom."

We walked on a bit in silence. I was thinking of the times I chose to spend with my dad - like that first date - in a period when kids used to say "never trust anyone over 30.'

"Your love for elderly people is admirable. You learned it from your Nana, and now you are able to reach out to your father."

We step up to a booth selling large juicy peaches and ripe plums. I think for a moment what might I offer this man whose arm I am holding. (Come to think of it, he does look a lot like my dad.) I select a peach and hold it out to him. He looks puzzled. Then I pull out a pocket knife and cut it into bite size pieces. I hand him one piece at a time as he slowly chews and swallows his way through the peach, savoring one juicy slice at a time. I understand that I need to pay attention to the quantity of wisdom I offer at any one time -- and not only with patients. I think about sending my dad one e-mail a day. Not my whole life and learning in one e-mail, and not all the things I am grateful for in one e-mail. No, I will send him small "slices" one each day to brighten his day and let him know how much I love him.

"That's it," the spirit says. "Nourish him daily, and in doing so you also will be nourished."

I hug the man and return to myself in my living room and put my drum down. I notice a tingling feeling in my heart as I think about my dad. How lovable he is!

In service to nourish the Heart, the Small Intestines in this point serves up usable quantities of joy.

Chapter 12: Linda and Harriet - Spirit Gate (Heart 7)

When I was still in my first year of practice in Florida, two patients came to me who were at opposite ends of the spectrum - so to speak. Linda was 7 months pregnant and Harriet was 85 years old.

Linda was temporarily living in Miami because her husband had a short term contract job. She didn't want to have her baby in California without her husband, so she came with him, set up house, found a midwife, and was referred to me by her acupuncturist in California (the same acupuncturist who had first treated me). For me as a new practitioner, Linda was magnificent to work with. She had been in treatment with a great practitioner for a number of years, she was awake to her body, and she had a harmonious outlook and understanding of her life.

Harriet came to me in order to quit smoking after fifty years of cigarettes. (Actually she never did quit.) She told me she had a boyfriend who was 87, and who came over a couple of times a week to spend the night. I was so delighted by her spirit! I used to treat her at her home, since she found driving through traffic to my office an ordeal.

After treating these two wonderful women for a couple of months, an amazing series of events occurred. I saw Harriet on a Monday. At that treatment, she told me that her boyfriend's daughter had told him that she relinquished any control over him, and she promised that when he was ready to go (die), she would not try to stop him. Harriet said she thought that was an incredible gift. She wished her daughter would do the same for her. Thursday, I got a call from Harriet's daughter to say that Harriet had had a heart attack and died. (I think that somehow she had known the time was close.) Her funeral was set for Saturday and I planned to go.

Life has a way of altering plans, however. Linda called on Saturday morning to say she was in labor. Since I had promised to be with her while the baby was born, I chose to miss the funeral. Harriet would have agreed, I knew.

Linda gave birth to a beautiful baby girl, while I received an early lesson about the profound job I get to do: That day was like standing in the gateway of life and death, a place that calls us away from the mundane obsessions that can fill our thoughts. When someone is dying, the last thing I think about is my bills or Facebook. And likewise, when a baby is being born, my focus stays here and now. I am overwhelmingly grateful that my work takes me to this sacred state of being completely present.

Spirit Gate - the journey

Spirit Gate is what we call a source point, meaning that if the meridian is a stream, the source point is the spring - source Qi (also called Yuan Qi) pools in these points - in this case, on the Heart meridian. The Heart is seen in Chinese medicine as the Supreme Controller. In other words, it speaks for the Divine or what is sometimes called the inner light. Accessing the source Qi of the Divine within us is an extremely powerful experience.

I enter the point, which is on the inside of the wrist just beside the wrist bone. The entrance feels like a small vortex, in which I spin around several times before I am once more on my feet, standing in a landscape that is flat and nondescript. The only obvious feature is an upright slab of solid iron. It takes me a minute to see that the slab is actually a gate, made solid to make it impermeable. On one side of the structure is a pool of water that stops at the gate. On its other side is a dry stream bed. When the gate is closed, no water gets through. When it is open, water either trickles or pours, depending on how wide the gate is opened. I look around for the spirit of the point.

"I am the spirit!" a voice bellows through my being. I look all around, but still see no one. "Well, open your eyes!" the voice bellows again, and I now see or sense that the voice is coming from the gate itself.

"*You* are the spirit of the point?"

"How many times do I have to tell you?" the gate harrumphs.

"Ok, I'm so sorry. Please, would you share with me the medicine or wisdom of this point?"

"Water is the source of all life, which is why you are about 75% water. The Earth's surface is also about 75% water, and this is no coincidence. My task, as you can see, is to allow the water to pass, in order to give life. I sometimes hold back the water, so as not to waste it. But this water is not physical water: it is the Qi of the spiritual waters. When a person's Spirit Gate is stuck closed, that person can have no vital spiritual life, but will be a walking, empty container. When the gate is stuck wide open, the person is ungrounded in physicality and will forget to take care of everyday things. When the gate is open just enough, there is balance. A steady flow of Source Qi animates and quickens people, making them present to the beauty and love in all of life, but also aware of the myriad of responsibilities they must handle day by day.

Having spoken, the gate opens about halfway so that water from the pool moves into the stream bed, gurgling and bubbling and singing as streams do. Released movement allows more water to arise from the source and refill the pool. The gate swings slightly, as needed to regulate the flow.

"Use this point," the gate continues, "when your patients are not open to the spiritual waters of the divine within themselves. You can also use this point when your patients are so open to the divine that they are unable to focus on everyday life." The gate slams shut as a large amount of water comes rushing up to the gate. As the water settles down a bit, the gate opens again slowly, little bit by little bit. The flow regulates again.

"Sometimes," the gate speaks, "too much Qi coming in can cause the person's spirit to be too active and not settled in, this causes your patients to experience insomnia. When everything is flowing smoothly, the person's spirit can rest. This point helps this regulation and invites their spirit to be settled."

I thank the gate and return to ordinary reality.

I think of Linda's baby, entering with the power of this gate of vital Qi, and I think of Harriet making her exit, having used the Yuan Qi to live her life. In the 25 plus years since these two patients, I have often had the joy and privilege of being with people while they die, and of being with new arrivals. Spirit Gate is in some ways the theme of the work we do as Acupuncturists, Shamans, Healers, or Midwives. The energy medicine of our needles can help a women's cervix open, or soothe pain in the back, or move a blockage of Qi that shows up as migraine. And very often these "physical" symptoms move only if emotional, mental, or spiritual blocks are first addressed. At some level, then, healing work consists of oiling and tending the Spirit Gate for our patients, clients and loved ones, and I love that. I am blessed that I get to help people birth and rebirth themselves; that I hold their hands as they experience the joys and sorrows of life and loss; that I go to their funerals and cry with their loved ones; that I mirror them, match them, and hold out possibility to them. And at the end of the day, I let them go. Then I wake up each new morning filled with joy and wonder about who I will get to see that day.

Chapter 13: Changes - Spirit Path (Heart 5)

It is hardly profound to say that everything changes. We all know. We know there are things that seem like constants in our lives, even as we also watch these constants change. Anyone who has been married for a long time has a sense of constancy in the relationship, even as they watched their spouses age, change hair styles, hair colors, body shape, clothing styles, habits, and even careers. They have watched their beloveds go from perfect eyes to reading glasses to bifocals, maybe trifocals. It all seems natural at the time: spouse as fixture. So we go along, creatures of habit, focusing on what we think won't change until changes smack us in the face - our beloved has a stroke or develops Alzheimer's! Then we are shocked out of denial.

I think about our ancestors. Did they think they would live forever when they were young and vibrant? When they took the world by the hand in revolution or civil war, did they think they were invincible? When women demanded the right to vote—and withstood incredible atrocities while imprisoned—did they think that one day they would be old and the young folks in their lives would be looking at them, thinking, *They don't know anything about revolution, they are just 'dumb old people.?*

Recently a young woman friend of mine, "Mandy," announced that she was quitting her job and moving out west. She has no job prospects - she just wants to live there. She said something like,"My parents are old and can't imagine how my generation can get in our cars and drive across the country." I wanted to laugh, because I love Mandy, and she is the same age as my daughter, and her parents are the same age as me. Well, when *I* was 19, I was at a festival in Ohio without a ride home to Los Angeles, so I jumped in a car with three strangers who were also going west. (We had pooled our money - $200 - and bought a clunker to make the drive.) And, If Mandy's parents think about it, I bet they also can remember doing something just that harebrained back at age 19. Somehow the Divine protects the innocent - most of the time. What I don't understand is how easily we forget, in the middle of life, what we did when we were young. And having forgotten, it's hard to watch when the young people we love take similar risks.

The Beatles reminded us that we all want to change the world, and I think that's true, and that we humans too often live in a paradox: we want to change the world, while also clinging to what we have. We think we can hold back the river of change, so we build bigger and stronger dams, but all the while, behind the dam the pressure builds, till one day the dam bursts. We don't wake up one day with heart disease or cancer. There have been signs - pressure on the dam - telling us that movement needs to occur.

What would our lives look like if we were able to embrace change as the tremendous gift that it is? How many of us stay in familiar, unhappy situations only because we are afraid to change?

In learning acupuncture, students are taught to notice how freely and unstoppably nature moves from one cycle to the next -- each day, each month, each season, and each year. The trees never say, "Nasty weather we're having," and you and I don't get to say, "I think I'll skip February this year." Nature moves and it's all good. Even our death serves. When we (or trees) die, we are making room for the young.

Once we have learned to observe changes in nature, and then in our bodies, and then in the fabric of our lives, without judgment, we can embrace change and be aware of the first small signs of dis-ease. That is why Chinese Medicine is sometimes thought of as preventative care. When people wake up to the subtle signals that their bodies send, they/we can make changes to allow movement instead of disease. For example, I have occasional neck pain. Once it's in full bloom, it can take weeks to get better. When I am awake to the subtleties my body tells me, however, I notice that in moments of stress I breathe more shallowly. After which it feels natural to elevate my shoulders and tense my muscles. Then if I hold that position for an hour or so - the length of a tense meeting, say - I clench my jaw. And then, within a few hours my neck locks up. Then I have to visit my chiropractor, massage therapist, and acupuncturist to get myself back in balance and out of pain. My body is smart, though. When I am listening to it, I am able to notice my shallow breathing, and then I take a moment to breathe deeply and step away from the stress. My "dam" doesn't burst and my neck doesn't lock up.

I have a patient, "Nick," who has been married for 15 years. The last 10 years have been most difficult for him. His wife has been sneaking around seeing another man (a friend of Nick's, no less), spending money the family cannot spare, refusing to get a job, and refusing to talk about any of it. Nick has tried everything he knows to help her, forgive her, open up to love with her, all to no avail. About six years ago, I asked him why he was staying in this situation. He said he didn't want to disrupt life for his children. I then asked him a question someone asked me before I left my first husband: "How can you raise healthy children in an unhealthy marriage?" He agreed with me. We have also talked about the ramifications for his health, as he always comes in for treatment, anxious, tense, angry, sad, etc.

Year after year Nick has tried to hold on to this ghastly marriage. Not only is he is now on medication for high cholesterol and high blood pressure, he has also developed a drinking problem. His dam is about to burst. As a practitioner, though, I can only ask questions.

Recently Nick asked his wife for a divorce, and they are working through a separation. He has some hard months ahead. I can see, happily, that he may be making this change early enough to avoid serious illness. What if his wife has been equally unhappy? What if her behavior has stemmed from the misery of looking across the room at someone who ought to be an intimate companion but is in some fundamental way incompatible?

I look around and see people by the millions who are sleep-walking through life. The planet is falling apart, the polar ice caps are melting, and whole species are dying everyday. Fellow humans are living on the streets, not knowing where their next meal will come from. Why does it take cataclysmic events (the dam bursting) to wake us up? Somehow, most folks assume they are safe and that nothing bad will ever happen to them -- until it does. That makes it hard to prepare for a difficult future.

At the same time, when a horrific change does occur - perhaps an earthquake, a hurricane, or a car accident, or even a gunner unloading anger on an innocent crowd -- people rouse and find that they have amazing strength to help one another cope. Think of the circles of people holding hands and singing in the streets of New York City after September 11, 2001; or the volunteers who sprang forward to help the wounded when the Boston Marathon was bombed; or the thousands of people helping New Yorkers after tropical storm Sandy; or the wealthy celebrities who have sent aid to Porto Rico. What if we could all be conscious more and more each day and be there for one another _without a disaster_?

We could do that. It is within us.

Spirit Path - the journey

As I enter the point on my arm, about an inch towards my elbow from Spirit Gate, I find myself walking down a dirt path. Buttercups and Pink Stork's Bills grow on both sides of the path. The flowers are singing, I think! I then look up and notice an intensely blue sky, blue, blue, blue, it has no clouds at all. I continue to move with my animal guide, not sure where I am going or who I will find. My guide communicates to me that I must remain awake and aware of everything. I notice grass - deep greens and light greens mixed. Though it's a warm and sunny day, the breeze is cool. Perfect weather for me? I feel as though I have made up this place. It's like a daydream! I even want to burst into song: "We're off to see the wizard!" I laugh to myself.

"What's so funny about that?" a voice sounds behind me. I turn around to see a character who looks like a jester, in a costume complete with bells on his two-pointed hat. He wears clown make-up as well. I ask, "Are you the spirit of this point?" He does a cartwheel, and as he springs up he says, "You know as well as I do that I am!"

"Can you tell me your medicine?"

"Spirit Path is not what you'd expect," he says. "It can look like this," -- he gestures to take in the idyllic day I have been experiencing -- "one minute, and then . . ." He waves his hand and suddenly it is pouring rain. Hail falls, the wind howls, and I am cold and sopping wet. He laughs and the storm vanishes.

We walk down the path side by side. "All paths are Spirit Path," he says. "Do you think you could ever get away from Spirit? Use this medicine when your patients are not aware of Spirit on their path. Wake them up with this point to the moment by moment life they are living." He pauses and holds a buttercup up to his chin. Yes, he likes butter. He drops the flower and starts again to walk.

"There are no mistakes," he says with emphasis: "When they have two or three or more paths to choose from, all paths are Spirit paths. This point will help them let go of the foolish idea that they 'should have' chosen a different path. Whatever paths they chose -- including the ones they will continue to choose -- are all Spirit paths. When dangers, disasters, or illness happen, it is all part of the experience. So are happiness and peace. Whatever happens, nothing is wrong: Spirit is still on the path with them."

At this he cartwheels out into the middle of the meadow, off the path where he first does a few quick somersaults and flip-flops, then sits on the grass with his legs spread in a "V." Grass and flower petals cling to his hat and he is laughing. I go over and sit beside him.

"So," he says. "Do you think 'off the path' is no longer Spirit Path?"

I know this is a trick question: I want to answer yes *and* no, but know that can't be right.

"Silly girl, don't you remember what I said earlier? Do you think you could ever get away from Spirit? Of course this is still Spirit Path. Paths are only started when someone is courageous enough to leave one path and forge a new one. Use this point for people who are asleep or no longer walking — stuck in the face of change. It will wake them up to the possibility of starting a new path, or of choosing to walk their present path with attention. It's all Spirit Path."

All paths are Sprit Path. I start to think about the patients I have who live in regret, wishing they had done something else, a different path. This will be a good point to remind them they have always been on Sprit Path.

Chapter 14: Sheri - Assembly of Ancestors (Three Heater 6)

Gratitude is a choice. Every experience, however "good" or "bad," can be received with gratitude or with negativity. One is always at choice, because not one of us escapes abuse, dysfunction, misunderstanding, heartache, heartbreak, loss, illness, and eventually death. In the midst of such pain, it can be near impossible to accept the lessons on offer. Later, though, we can develop the ability to see both the lessons and the gifts that each painful experience brings — not that it's easy. No one can promise life will be easy.

"Sheri" first came to me for neck pain, but she stopped coming after four acupuncture treatments. I didn't know whether she'd been helped, until a few years later, when she called out of the blue and said she had stage four breast cancer. She told me that the original treatments had helped her neck so much that now she was hoping acupuncture could help her with the side effects of chemo. Once we started treatment, she began to ask questions about shamanism, and soon she was taking my classes and participating in my drumming group. The community of people in the drumming group and classes embraced Sheri and she them.

After surgery, chemotherapy, and radiation, Sheri enjoyed about a year without cancer. Then it came back, spreading through her spine and bones. In her last few months of life, she was in a great deal of pain. Sheri was only in her mid thirties and was so angry at the prospect of death that she alienated most of her "regular" friends. The healing community took up collections to help her financially, however, and one woman from the drumming group spent three days a week with Sheri — every week, no matter what. Her love and stamina were powerful.

During the time of wellness before her death, Sheri became a dear friend to me. She helped me organize my classes; she traveled to Santa Fe when I took classes there, both to keep me company and also to help me endure my fear of flying. She took in my daughter and me when we left my second husband. In every way, I am so grateful for the friendship we had. Sadly, Sheri passed away at age 39, nine days before Christmas.

Ten days before her death, three of us went to see Sheri in her hospice room. We did a shamanic journey with her, the intention being to help her see who would meet her when she died. She saw a friend who had died of cancer a few years before, and also her dog, who had died two years previously; both were waiting for her on the beach. After that journey, Sheri, who had been agitated and fearful, became accepting and peaceful. The hospice staff commented on the shift, and her relatives were amazed at Sheri's new calm.

At her memorial service, I invited people to share stories from their life with Sheri, most of which were funny. That was natural, as Sheri had an incredible sense of humor, and the laughter that filled the room brought a real sense of her presence. In gratitude I remember Sheri's laughter, the way she could transform a situation from serious and depressing to funny and ridiculous. In gratitude I hold my friend's light in the depth of my being. I may have been older than she, but she was a teacher for me. I consider her one of my "ancestor" spirits.

Assembly of Ancestors - the journey

As I entered the point, about three inches from my wrist towards my elbow on the outside of my arm, I walked into a circle of women sitting around a fire. One woman was tending the fire, tossing in herbs and bowing in reverence to it. The smoke smelled like sage and tobacco. Hmm. Odd. This gathering seemed more Native American than Chinese.

"Ancestors from all traditions are represented here," said the woman in the center, reading my thoughts. "This circle exists within each of us, and gives each of us universal wisdom." She placed another log on the fire as I walked over to join her.

The warmth from the fire reminds me of the function of this Meridian/Official, which is to maintain and circulate the warmth of the body -- and spirit, no doubt. I look around the circle and see women of many ethnicities, colors, shapes and ages - including my friend Sheri! As I puzzled over her presence, the woman in the center said, "Each person that touches you in a deep way becomes a teacher or ancestor for you. When they die and you add their wisdom to your own, you embody them."

"Are you the spirit of this point?" I ask her.

"Yes, I am." She looks over at Sheri and beckons her to join us. "The medicine of this point is about remembering what you know inside yourself. And since every person and every situation you meet adds to the circle, periodically visiting this point with patients encourages them to access their wisdom even as they continue to acquire it."

She turns to Sheri who has now joined us, and I feel tears welling up. I miss her terribly. "Your friend had much to teach you about yourself," says the woman to me, "and so now she sits with the ancestors in your heart. You can rely on her wisdom to be with you always."

Sheri embraced me in a new way. In life, her hugs had been near ceremonial; she could not embrace fully due to the pain from her mastectomy. Here and now she was no longer in pain, and she embraced me with her whole strength. She reminded me that all problems in life are manageable so long as I can laugh.

The woman in the center told me to bring people to this point frequently. "Assembly of Ancestors will remind them that they know what they know. Our personal circle of ancestors grows as long as we live."

I return to myself and turn off the drumming CD.

I am not sure why my personal circle of ancestors is made up of women only; it may have something to do with my shamanic lineage. In any event, most people's circles tend to be more mixed. I tell patients that their circle is their own, accumulated over a lifetime, and I invite them to explore who is there. People from the deep past, whom we knew perhaps in childhood, are often prominent in the circle.

At a class I once taught, Sheri was present when we were discussing our next class, which was to include a sweat lodge. Briefly: a sweat lodge is a temporary structure, usually made of tree branches covered with blankets, with a pile of red-hot stones in the center. Once you are inside, the door (a flap of a blanket) is closed. The space is pitch dark, lit only by the glow of the rocks. The shaman then pours water on the rocks to create steam and may burn herbs as well, all in aid of sacrifice, prayer, letting go of toxins, entering the womb of the earth, and coming out reborn. The question asked was prosaic: what do people wear in a sweat lodge? Of course, Native Americans traditionally go naked in a sweat lodge, but I knew middle class Americans wouldn't go for that, so I suggested shorts and tee shirts. One person jokingly suggested wearing thongs with the fur of our power animals, and we all laughed.

The following week, Sheri and I went out to study with Sandra Ingerman in New Mexico, and while I was studying, Sheri went shopping: she bought a thong for each person in the class. Even though she was too sick to undergo a sweat lodge, she packaged each one in a small brown bag and asked me to pass them out to the class. The laughter lasted long into the next month when one student sent an email to us all saying that his wife loved the thong (on him) and thanked Sheri. He brought his thong with him (in his pocket) to Sheri's memorial service to remind us all of Sheri's powerful gift of humor.

Wisdom comes in many forms, and I am grateful for the wisdom of humor Sheri gave us all, and I know that in my circle of ancestors she is undoubtedly telling raunchy jokes to the group, and they're falling over laughing by the fire. Ho! Sheri!

Section 5: Late Summer

I cannot lie to you: Late Summer is my least favorite time of year. The heat and humidity zap my energy and I find myself praying for Fall to come. Doing anything outside is really out of the question. When I try, I walk around with wet clothes and wet hair. I can, however, talk about the gifts and virtues of this season.

The Chinese distinguish the Late Summer as separate from Summer because it is the time of harvest. Everything has matured so now it is time to gather the fruits of our labor. Fruit and vegetable stands spring up along country roads, and the Farmer's Markets overflow with a bounty that is the one thing I love about this season. Blackberries! Peaches! Cucumbers, plums and more, more, more tomatoes. It is so easy to eat healthfully in late summer.

The sunsets are magnificent at this time of year, because the humidity in the air reflects light and constitutes more substance to be illuminated. People have barbecues and pool parties to share the bounty. This is the time people do their canning and display their products at state and county fairs. Nature is so ripe, there is often fruit rotting on the ground — which is actually part of the universal plan. When seeds fall to the earth, they give rise to future harvests.

When you think of late summer, think of sweetness, ripeness, fullness, and harvest. The emotion is sympathy - a quality that in western culture is akin to pity. Needless to say, the ancient Chinese meant something far deeper. When my kids were little, my mother used to tell me how much more fun it was to be a grandmother than a parent. I laughed at her a bit and I didn't really get it until recently, when I volunteered to be the "grandmother" for a young mother I know. I had offered to watch the baby so my friend and her husband could have some alone time. I'd have the baby for about six hours. Well! I spent the whole six hours doing nothing but holding, feeding, and loving this baby. I now knew the difference. As a young mother, I always had so many other responsibilities — like shopping, cleaning, cooking, laundry, the list goes on and on — that I was always waiting for the babies to go to sleep so I could get my "work." I never took the time to just deeply enjoy my babies, simply smelling them and touching them and watching them meet the world.

But now, because I knew my time with the baby had a limit, there was nothing else I "had" to do other than to savor every moment with the baby — and here we are in Late Summer. I would say that *savoring,* far more than sympathy, is the emotion of late summer. Savoring says, "I am with you, I've got you, nothing else is more important or needs to be done other than being with you." In this emotion we are thoughtful, focused on sussing out what the other needs and how best to provide it. In this mindset we are understanding, empathic, and compassionate.

Late summer is not a fast energy; it is an embracing, caring, "grandmotherly" energy. I think of my grandmother and how she listened to me and took me in exactly as I was. She didn't try to fix me or tell me what to do. She simply held me in love. Such is the way of Late Summer. (You will meet my grandmother in one chapter of this section.)

The element of the season is Earth, and its organs/officials are the Stomach and Spleen - which makes sense as these organs handle harvest, nourishment, and sweetness. The Stomach takes in the nourishment, rots and ripens it, then passes the essence to the Spleen to be delivered throughout the body. The Stomach processes *all* that we take in, be it physical, mental, or emotional. If you have ever heard someone say, "I just can't stomach any more of this," then you have heard from the official of this season and the emotional/mental process it provides.

When you next experience Late Summer, ask yourself, "Have the plans that I made in Spring matured in the Summer? Have they brought me a harvest? Can I move into Autumn knowing what is valuable and what needs to be pruned?" Make an assessment as you look at your bounty, and give yourself a hearty pat on the back for a job well done.

Chapter 15: Did you say Faeries?: Abundant Splendor - (Stomach 40)

Do I believe in Faeries? Well, I'm going to pull an "Irish one" on the reader: yes *and* no. In Celtic legends there is a distinction between what they call Faeries and what the American-Disney culture thinks of as Faeries. Disney's cute little winged nymph-like flower faeries are what the Celts would call nature spirits. Faeries according to Celtic beliefs are human sized, benign and lordly beings who mirror our culture without the destructive tendencies.

I once spent ten days in Ireland, traveling around in a class on Celtic Shamanism. Our guide and teacher (Tom Cowan, author of *Fire in the Head: Shamanism and the Celtic* Spirit) would tell stories and legends, many of which ended with "and they slipped through the crevices between the rocks and landed in Faerie-land, never to be heard from again."

Benign they may be, but the Faeries had a mischievous side as well; they are known for luring folks into their realms and keeping them for what seems like a night but turns out to be years. Rip Van Winkle is an example. So is Morgan Le Fey, a character in *Mists of Avalon* by Marion Zimmer Bradley, who spends five years in the Faerie realm and does not age. Former guests of the Faeries often find that they have not aged, though everyone they knew is old or dead.

Faeries are very much connected with the land, and it was considered an honor to the Faeries to honor the land. Tom Cowan said that there were two times of year when the Faeries changed "camps"; in the Fall they would go to their Winter camp, and in the Spring they would go to their Summer camp. As they were moved across the land, people were expected to put out food for them, to honor them. If they did the, Faeries blessed their households. If they failed to honor, Tom said, "the Faeries would shit in their wine vats."

What Faeries represent to me is the idea of how Spirit intends us to live. Instead of focusing on greed - money at all cost - we should live in the joy of the land, in harmony with nature, and retain our youthful abandon and playful mischief. I think that is what the Faeries are supposed to represent for us. Tom also said it was once common to ask someone if they had Faerie blood (in their ancestry). What that question says to me is, do you have a connection with the spirits in nature? Can you play hard and love strong and have fun?

This point brings me to my youngest daughter. When she was little she was, like most children, happy in nature. At the time we moved to Maryland, she was nine years old, blond, blue-eyed, and full of impish charm. We moved in next door to a family with triplet girls, who were five years old at the time, and they too were blond and blue-eyed. The triplets saw my daughter as their long-lost big sister, and she in turn saw them as three little versions of herself to boss around. What fun! Their parents, however, were very much a product of the "yuppie" culture. Dad was a hard working professional, while Mom stayed home with the girls. I watched as they had immaculate new sod installed in their already sculptured yard, while our yard supported the treasured "weeds" that all house witches and faeries love. My daughter quickly fell out of grace with the triplets' parents, who asked her not to visit.

Nevertheless, when our first spring in that neighborhood arrived, one Saturday morning I was awakened by voices in the yard. I heard the triplets squealing with delight as they asked my daughter (through the fence) what she was doing. They sounded like a litter of kittens, with their adorable, high-pitched voices. She answered that she was blowing wishes and she proceeded to blow the cotton-like head of an old dandelion and watch the seeds float away on the air. Jumping up and down in their own yard, the three little girls giggled and squealed that they too wanted to blow wishes. My daughter thought all kids should be allowed to blow wishes, so she went about gathering dandelion puff balls and passing them through the fence so the triplets could "blow wishes" all over their parents perfect yard. Faerie mischief at its best!

Of course, I stopped her, but in my own mind I think . . . Who decided that dandelions are weeds? Dandelions have numerous medicinal qualities: a powerful diuretic, a high level of potassium - that sounds like a good choice against fluid retention to me. Dandelions are a gift!

The thing about our beautiful, magnificent world is that everything we need is here, provided for us and the "Faerie" part of us knows it's all there for the noticing. I say that we are all born with "Faerie" as our spirit, but that too many have given their spirit away in pursuit of things, believing that "There isn't enough to go around." We have forgotten that all around us is Abundant Splendor.

Abundant Splendor - the journey

I enter the point, Abundant Splendor, on the front of my leg midway between knee and ankle, to find myself standing in tall grasses. I am looking around for the spirit of the point when my animal guide points at the ground, where I see a grasshopper. I ask, "Is this the spirit of the point?" and he says yes. He tells me to shrink myself to the size of the grasshopper, so I do, and Grasshopper tells me to climb onto his back. We take off.

Whee! It is a wild ride, a lot more fun than I would have guessed. We go sailing over the grasses and land between them, then sail again. Finally we stop beside a tall dandelion. I climb off Grasshopper's back and he begins munching on the dandelion leaves.

He says, "Such a feast!"

I start munching as well. All around me are plants of every sort, and because I am so small, I can also see all kinds of critters munching on the dandelions, grasses, and other plants.

Grasshopper turns to me and speaks. "When you think of Abundant Splendor, what comes to your mind?"

"I always picture a large scene like the Grand Canyon, or maybe a mountain vista."

"Precisely. Like you, most people think that *abundance* or *splendor* must be on a large scale, so they miss the simple *abundance* all around them. I exist to remind your patients that everything from the very small to the very large is "Abundant Splendor." This point is about gratitude. When you are awake to the abundance all around you, the result can only be gratitude. Look for an awareness of gratitude when you use this point on your patients."

I climb back on his back and he returns me to my guide. I am filled with gratitude.

"Thank you, Grasshopper, for the abundantly fun ride, and for showing me the abundance all around." I am moved to tears.

Grasshopper changes form into a large man, dressed like a southern gentleman from the 1800s, complete with a black top hat. He removes an immaculate white handkerchief from his shirt pocket and gently wipes my tears. "I am obliged to be of service, ma'am." I am tickled by this form of address and smile at him, through my tears. I bid him good-bye and leave.

Chapter 16: Gloria and Lillian - Three Yin Crossing: (Spleen 6)

A few years after I moved to Maryland I began treating a teenage boy who was on both Ritalin and Prozac. He had been diagnosed as having ADHD in grade school, and then the previous summer, between his junior and senior year of high school, he went into a deep depression and refused to come out of his room. His doctor put him on Prozac for the depression, with the promise that once he got over the hump his parents could take him off it. Then a few months down the road, when his parents wanted to take him off Prozac, the doctor didn't want to "rock the boat." Frustrated, his parents decided to try an alternative approach -- acupuncture. Tim was a very smart and creative young man, and within six months he was off all medication and doing well. He went on to culinary school and is now a chef in a very upscale restaurant in New York City.

I bring up Tim because I immediately felt a friendship or kinship with his mother, Gloria. Gloria is a librarian and a very strong and intelligent woman. I looked forward to chatting with Gloria every time she brought Tim to the office, and after a while she and I, with her friend, Lillian, started a book group. The three of us met one morning a week for several years to read together: *Conversations with God,* by Neale Donald Walsh, *The Tao of Pooh, The Te of Piglet,* by Benjamin Hoff and a few others.

We took turns meeting at one another's homes and served breakfast. What grew out of these meetings was a strong and supportive friendship. We talked about our issues with our husbands and our children. We came to each others parties; we had dinners with each others families or spouses. They were my rock.

When I had to go to New York for a class that coincided with my older daughter's prom, Lillian helped her get dressed and videotaped the ritual "send off" for me. When Lillian and her husband needed to get a way for a weekend, her daughter stayed with us, and so on. Eventually, both women moved away -- Lillian out west and Gloria down south -- but for those years their friendship was like gold to me. Sadly, we have not stayed in touch. I wonder about them every once in a while and hope they are well and happy.

The point where our paths crossed was the exact time we all needed them to cross. It was like a point on the inside of the shin called, "Three Yin Crossing." In some cases yin can be described as feminine. Lillian, Gloria, and I were the three "yin" whose paths crossed, a junction that helped us walk our lives.

Three Yin Crossing - the journey

I sink into the point on the inside of my shin and find myself in a warm dining room. There are three women, who seem ageless to me, sitting at the table. They are very different from each other, one with dark brown almost black hair, and cold grey/blue eyes, one with soft ginger hair, green eyes and freckles, the other with light brown hair and brown eyes and a dark tan. The one with ginger hair exclaims, "She's here, she's here!" I look around before I realize she is talking about me. The table is spread with hot coffee, juicy, ripe cantaloupe, and warm buttery croissants.

I introduce myself and ask which one is the spirit of the point. They all say in chorus, "I am." Smiling, I ask for their medicine.

Immediately I find myself in a room where a woman is giving birth. It is a home birth in a house with a thatched roof, in what appears to be an English village. Only women are present - the three women I had just met, to be exact. They are assisting the birth. When the baby comes, they clear his airway, wrap him in a blanket, and hand him to the mom. Then they matter-of-factly clean her up.

One of them turns to me and says, "We are the midwives of all birthing."

Next we are in the forest with a group of teenage girls. Several of them are having their first periods, and the three women are explaining menstruation and sex to the girls. They seem awed at becoming <u>women,</u> no longer <u>girls.</u> One of the group is not only having her first period, but is also engaged to be married, letting me know that this scene to came from a time in the past (she was 13 or 14 years old at most.)

Another of the women turns to me to say, "We are the educators of young women."

Next we find ourselves at the bedside of a dying woman. A fire burns in the fireplace and the three women are wiping her face and helping her sip water. They have little glass vials of potions they are using to ease her pain.

The third woman looks at me and says, "We are here to help her transition. This is another form of midwifery."

We are back in the dining room. The first woman says to me, "Use this point for rites of passages for women. Women need women to support and help them through the changes of life. In your culture, women are isolated by their jobs and individual homes, whereas in the past, we used to be *village* people. We all watched each other's children, and we helped each other pass through marriage, birth, menstruation, and death. Now women are attempting to live as men do. The feminine is missing."

"You can use this point on men too, for men in your time have lost access to their feminine, nurturing energy. They are even ashamed of it! This point, Three Yin Crossing, brings home the feminine and helps all patients know they have the feminine support they need."

Each in turn gives me a long, strong hug, and I return to myself.

When I think of those years with Gloria and Lillian and the many heart-to-heart talks we had, I am extremely grateful. Gloria, strong and powerful with an informed and righteous indignation for the atrocities being perpetrated on women in Afghanistan and Iraq. Lillian, creative and inventive, running a business out of her home so she could be home for her teenage daughters. My life took a turn that led to a traumatic divorce, and my daughters and I would not have made it through without Lillian and Gloria. My yin crossing was only possible because of these wonderful friends.

Chapter 17: Miracles and Grandmothers - Supreme White: (Spleen 3)

Some say there is no such thing as a miracle.

I disagree. When I leave the house every summer morning and see the morning glories on my fence, the words that come to mind are "miracle" and "Nana."

My grandmother, my Nana, loved morning glories. I remember her standing in our back yard in Texas (where my father was stationed at the time), with the wind blowing her gray hair. She was pinning clothes on the line and pointing out the morning glories, which were just beginning to unfurl. To this day I can't look at a morning glory without thinking of my grandmother. The miracle is that I feel her love for me even though she has been dead for many years now.

Nana actually lived with us in Texas, and part of that time she shared a room with me. She taught me bible verses and listened to me sing. I loved to sing. It didn't matter that I couldn't carry a tune, the songs I sang were unrecognizable. Nana acted like I was the best singer she'd ever heard.

My grandmother had been adopted at the age of 5 by a wealthy family who apparently wanted a pretty little girl to dress up and show off. They actually changed her name to Gladys; I don't know what her original name was. They got more than they bargained for, as my grandmother turned out to be sickly. I believe she said she never got further than 7th or 8th grade; at one point she missed an entire year due to illness. My mother and I think she may have been sexually abused, judging from memories that surfaced in her late-life dementia. Gladys married in her late 20s, a bit later than was usual in those days, and her adopted parents didn't like her choice of husbands. They disowned her.

The thing I find most puzzling in her story is that her mother could give her up for adoption at the age of 5, as we know she did. This happened long before the depression, when that sort of thing happened frequently. As a mother myself, I remember that my first child was unplanned, and that I had considered adoption, but once I held her in my arms and looked into her eyes, I was completely in love. What could have happened to my great-grandmother that she let go of her 5-year-old? Was her life <u>so</u> hard? Did she suffer a disharmony of soul? Or was it love for this child that motivated giving her up? Perhaps she thought that giving her daughter to a wealthy family would guarantee a happier life.

Gladys had twin boys who died at birth, full term. (I can't begin to fathom the pain.) Then at age 38, in 1940, she had my mother by cesarean section. In America, c-sections are now routine, but in 1940 it was a major, major operation. She apparently didn't recover for a long time, if ever. In 1951, my grandfather left her and my mother to run off to California with a woman who was 20 years younger than he. This woman, whom he later married, left her own husband and four daughters.

As for my grandmother, child support laws were not yet in effect, and her adoptive parents still would have nothing to do with her. Having no professional skills, Nana then supported herself and my mother by taking jobs as a nanny. She would be gone all week, only home on the weekends, leaving my mother (aged 11) to fend for herself. She had no other choice, so my mother had to grow up fast: she quit school at age 14 to go to work, met my father at not quite 16, got married three weeks before she turned 17, and gave birth to me 13 months later.

Knowing my grandmother and the amazing unconditional love she gave me brings me to the next part of her story. Given the chill of her adoptive family, it makes sense that she must have experienced a powerful love before her adoption. How else could she *give* such love? So she had some type of a loving beginning. How, then, must her natural grandmother (my great-great grandmother) have felt about the adoption? Was she angry with her daughter? Was she bereft at losing the child? I believe she was. From what happened next, I know that my grandmother lit up her world?

When my grandmother died I was 37. I went to bed that night, very sad after my mother's phone call, and also relieved. Nana had been in a nursing home for 5 years unable to recognize any of us. The next morning when I woke, however, I couldn't move my neck, which hurt excruciatingly. Driving was actually dangerous. I saw a chiropractor, and manipulation helped my neck. But then within a few months I started having panic attacks, and my lifelong fear of heights became so strong that I couldn't drive over bridges. Eventually, I sought the help of a shaman, and we discovered that Gladys' grandmother's spirit had come to live with me when I was small, so that she could be close to her granddaughter. Since Nana and I had been close, I was a perfect host for her. Now that Nana was dead, she no longer needed a host, and so she started creating physical problems for me so that I would seek help to let her go. The shaman helped me create a link by which she could leave me and move on to be with Nana in another plane.

To this day, when I need help with relationship issues, I visit Nana and her grandmother in a shamanic journey, where they wait for me in a cute little cottage with blue morning glories all around the fence. I enter their sun-drenched cottage and sit in the "Florida room" on wicker furniture, and they serve me tea and cookies. I invite the higher self of whomever I'm in conflict with into this place and we talk with the help of the grandmothers. I am always amazed at how this process shifts things in ordinary reality.

And that is why the miracle of morning glories fills me with the love of Nana and her grandmother. I have no doubt that someday my granddaughter (who has just manifested in this world on Jan 5, 2016) will be drawn to morning glories and will visit the same cottage in the upper world to speak with me and my grandmother and my great-great grandmother for the wisdom of the wise women we are.

Supreme White - the journey

In the comfort of my living room with the drumming CD, I enter the point (it is just under the knobby bone on the inner side of the foot), Supreme White, and emerge in a medieval-looking village; there are a few shops, crooked streets of houses, children playing, cats, horses, carts, all surrounded by a deep, dark forest. It looks European. Wandering through the village, I am looking around for the spirit of this point, when suddenly I see a hut near the edge of the woods. The sign over the door actually says, "Supreme White"!

This makes me laugh as I walk to the hut and knock on the door. A female voice tells me to come in. When I walk in, I see an old woman with long white hair sitting by the fireplace. I ask if she is the spirit of this point, and she says she is. She adds," Can't you tell? I have white hair." She laughs. She stands up and opens an herb jar and puts a pinch into a cauldron that is cooking on the fire. She stirs it and tastes it.

She says, "It's almost ready. Come in and close the door, and tell your animal to lie on the floor."

So we do. It is very cozy and warm by the fire. She asks me what I want, and I say I want to learn the wisdom of this point, Supreme White. She laughs again.

The woman speaks slowly, thinking as she speaks. She says, "I am old and wise. I have seen many things and I know many things. I've experienced many things. I've helped many people, and the people of this village respect me. They come to me when they need help, or when they need answers, or when they need instructions. The medicine of this point will help your patients find their own internal equivalent of me. In that way the medicine reminds us to respect the elder part of our consciousness. This point will help those who think they are worse off because they are getting older. It will help them find *delight* in their old age. But come, let me show you more." She stands up and goes to the door. We walk outside and down a narrow path into the forest.

As she walks, I notice that her long white hair is in a beautiful plait down her back, with flowers braided into it. The braid is thick and reaches to her knees, a gorgeous, solid white that glows when a sunbeam hits it. As we walk, we come to a stream with a little bridge, then we walk across it into tall trees and to the center of a clearing. (Tom Cowan would say the Gaelic word for a clearing in the woods - a nemeton.) Out of her little bag, my companion pulls a blanket, which she spreads out on the floor of the forest and tells me to have a seat, so we sit down.

She says, "The ancient wisdom of this point resides in its connection with trees. The trees are tall and strong and their roots reach down deep into the Earth. It is no accident that this point nearly touches the ground when we walk, because that contact helps us find the wisdom of the Earth, the true ancient mother. Earth is the mother who has nurtured us and supported us, the one who has held us since day one - also the one we neglect, the one we forget about - and also the one we modern people abuse. And we abuse her within ourselves, too. In fact, if we didn't abuse Earth within ourselves, we would likely not abuse her in the world. This point will help those who abuse the Earth within themselves to stop that abuse. It will help them recognize their deep, deep roots within the Earth."

She looks around and seeing mushrooms beneath the trees, she goes over and gathers some. "These mushrooms are wonderful for stews," she says, and she puts them in her bag. Then she finds and picks some wild onions. She tells me, "These also will go perfectly in the stew I am cooking in my home."

She says, "Before we leave this spot, I want you to lie down on the Earth and feel the strength, the solidness, and the support. You don't have to worry about falling from the forest floor, and this point is like that too. There's no need to worry about falling. Earth has got us. She <u>holds</u> us."

The ground is cool as I lie there, and soon I feel myself sinking into the ground. I become part of the ground. I am the Earth. I feel the earthworms moving through me. I feel the tree roots giving me structure. I remember the plants growing up through me, and the dying leaves decomposing and becoming part of me. I remember people sitting on me. I am almost lost to myself, as I have become the Earth and the soil and minerals, when Supreme White shakes my arm to bring me back.

We walk back in silence, moving slowly towards the hut. She stops on the way to wash the onions and mushrooms in the stream. When we are back inside, she cuts them up and puts them in the stew and stirs it. We sit quietly, listening to the simmering of the stew. I notice the strong, delicious aroma. Finally, she ladles some into a mug. As I savor the stew on my tongue, the flavor is earthy, solid and dense. I feel as if I'm eating the soil itself. The taste is both slightly salty and slightly sweet, and as I eat, I feel a warm calmness spreading through my body. I feel supported, nurtured, and connected with the Earth.

The old woman now shapes some symbols in the air with her hands, then places her hands on my cheeks and says, "Daughter, you are of the earth, just as I am, and one day you will grow to be a Supreme White. Your hair will grow long and white, and those who know you will come, and learn from you. When you use this point for your patients, be aware that this point is also part of who you are. Within you is not only your child self, not only your modern day self, but also your someday self, who is old and white and full of the wisdom of the Earth and the ancestors. When you use this point with your patients, know that you are bringing all the generations into the needle to help them remember that they, too, embody all the generations before and after them."

My power animal says it is time to go, I stand and embrace Supreme White and thank her for stew and her message. We leave the way we came.

I hold the wisdom of Nana and her grandmother in my consciousness when I use this point. I know that they and their struggles - and their perseverance - are part of me. I am Supreme White, with their help, when I offer this point to my patients.

Chapter 18: Cindy and Earth Granary - (Stomach 4)

My friend Cindy lives out on the side of a mountain, in the Shenandoah Valley, in a farm house built in the 18th century. She lives with her "boyfriend." (They have lived together for several decades and she still refers to him as her boyfriend. I find that sweet.) Cindy is fearless. She says exactly what she thinks and never seems to worry what other people think of her.

Knowing I wanted deer rib bones to make a rattle, Cindy called me and said she had been watching a deer carcass for a while and thought it was ready to be "harvested." I drove out the following weekend, and for dinner we ate venison and fresh vegetables from her garden. In the morning we hiked to a waterfall, which was at least two stories high and cascaded into a brook. We could hear both the crash and the gurgle long before we could see the fall itself, and when we got there, spray filled the air, giving the fall a mystical aura. Earth and Water in all their glory!

In the afternoon, we drove to the carcass and used trash bags to haul it back to Cindy's house. Oh boy, did it stink! (I was worried the smell would stay in my car.) Because of the smell, we worked in the yard, and it was hard, unpleasant labor. We needed to cut the ribcage from the rest of the bones, but the ligaments were still attached and put up a mighty fight.

Ligaments are tough. It was as though they wanted to stay with the bones. Cindy's boyfriend, Paul, came out to help, until at some point a gazillion death beetles came pouring out of this stinky, nasty mess. Paul's face turned gray and he was done. He couldn't help anymore. Quite honestly, I was ready to take the body back to where we got it, but Cindy was unstoppable. She continued to work, while I was swallowing bile and doing my best. We finally got the ribs cut apart and packaged in plastic for me to take home. (Now I was worried about the _beetles_ getting into my car.)

Cindy and I have had some fun times together, starting the moment we met: she decided to take my two year shamanism course from a flyer she found at a retreat center in West Virginia. But before signing up, she came out to meet me by attending my intro course. Afterwards we went out for lunch. We were intending some serious talk, only first we spent about half an hour exchanging jokes. We were laughing hard . . .

Cindy has taken a lot of my classes since that time and eventually assisted me in teaching. We also attended the two year teacher's training course with Sandra Ingerman at the Omega Institute, in upstate New York, together. We would often meet in Pennsylvania and ride the rest of the way together, leaving one car with a friend.

One of the things I admire most about Cindy is her all-around strength -- not only in the face of stinks, but in the face of whatever comes: she is like a modern day pioneer woman. She and Paul grow a huge garden, with tomatoes, bell peppers, corn, and more. They sell some produce at the local farmer's market, and Cindy makes pans and pans and pans of stuffed bell peppers and freezes them to eat all winter. She makes tomato sauce and cans it. She works hard, not only for survival but also as a massage therapist and healer. When I visit her farm, there is always a "herd" of kitties who are well loved and well fed. Nothing at all seems too big for Cindy to tackle. She is basically self-sufficient. Whenever I visit Cindy and Paul, no matter the time of year, there is always a bountiful feast.

Earth Granary - the journey

I sit down with my drum and begin the "second nature" monotonous rhythm that takes me on my journey inward. I enter the point (it is located one on either side of the mouth) and slide down a tunnel. When I land, it is on something soft -- grain, as it turns out: I am inside a granary -- a storehouse. The many tall piles of grain have been husked, but are not yet flour. Each grain is distinct. I see a woman with a pitchfork entering the storehouse, who sees me and points the pitchfork at me. She is dressed in overalls, and a short sleeved tee shirt.

Her hay colored hair is pulled back in one pony tail behind her neck. She is sweaty and dirty.

"You come down here!" she hollers, shaking the fork for emphasis.

I climb down and brush the grain off my clothes. "Are you the spirit of this point?" I ask.

She replies, "Who were you expecting, Gandhi?"

"I really wasn't expecting anyone in particular," I say, a little afraid of this woman.

"Well, you best be following me," she said, as she leaned the pitchfork against the wall and opened the door. We walked outside, where there were fields of grain, blowing in the breeze for as far as I could see. There were also many more granaries, places where the harvest is kept clean and free of pests. "The earth can produce enough food for everyone," she said. "The problem is that only a few people know that. It's the same within a person. People have all the Qi they need, but often without noticing. Treating this point shows people the limitless fields of grain. It reassures them they have a gracious plenty, all stored for use as needed."

We walked to the edge of the nearest field and she plucked a stem of wheat and handed it to me. "It is one thing to have all you need and another thing to have it in a form that can be used. A granary isn't just about storing grain - it is about harvesting and processing the grain for storage and/or use. Take your patients to this point when they don't know what they have, or if they don't know how to process what they have -- which isn't always easy, mind you. But anyway, this point will show them their own abundance." She turned me toward the storehouse I came from and gave me a little shove. "Scamper along, now."

I went into the storehouse and asked my power animal to bring me back, and he did.

Earth Granary reminds me of Cindy, who year after year continues to plant, harvest, and process her food. Her home is in one of the most beautiful places in our country. (John Denver even wrote a song about the area!) Cindy works hard and lives simply, mistress of great riches!

Section 6: Oceans

There are two major energy pathways (also called "meridians") that do not align with the seasons, nor are they bilateral. One is Yin and the other is Yang. The Yin meridian rises up the center of the front of the body, while the Yang goes up the backbone. Both have deep branching pathways that connect them with each other in such a way that when viewed from the side, the pattern looks like a figure eight. (Or when the person is lying down, it looks like an infinity symbol. Imagine that!)

These two meridians are referred to as Oceans which are both the source and end-point of water on this planet. In the body, likewise, the Oceans are so fundamental if there is a block between them, none of the other meridians will have the Qi they need -- so much so that the practitioner will literally have difficulty feeling the patient's pulses: Given the block, pulses get that faint. In such a case, the practitioner can treat the bilateral meridians till she is "blue in the face," to no effect. Nothing can shift until any block between the Oceans is cleared.

The meridian in the front of the body is called the Conception Vessel and is Yin in nature. Of the two, Yin is more feminine, relates to evening/night time, and is passive. The meridian on the back is called the Governor Vessel, and it is more Yang in nature. Yang is more masculine, relates to the day time, and is more aggressive. Yin and Yang together are sometimes described as "the dark side of the hill" and the "sunny side of the hill," a metaphor that points to their essential unity. Yin and Yang are different aspects of what Is, in this case, a single hill. There can be no Yin without Yang, nor Yang without Yin.

I have chosen two points, one from each Ocean, to journey to and to write about. The important thing for you to remember is that while these special meridians are not associated with any particular season, they do feed the bilateral meridians, and therefore have profound effects on the seasons within the body, mind and spirit.

Chapter 19: Jamie and Dove Tail - (Conception Vessel 15)

"Jamie" came to me three weeks after the death of his 17-year-old daughter, "Carly." He wanted me to do a Shamanic healing session with him. Carly was the oldest of Jamie's three children, a fun and funny girl with lots of friends and a strong sense of adventure. Jamie told me that once when he took her to New Zealand, she insisted on going sky diving -- something Jamie himself was terrified to do. Not wanting to discourage her, however, he said okay and they did it together. He has shown me pictures.

On that particular Halloween, Carly had gone out with friends and "huffed" canned air to get high. The canned air has a propellant that apparently exacerbated a heart arrhythmia Carly had had from birth, causing her to go into fibrillation. She came home and went to bed, had a heart attack, and died in her sleep. Jamie and his wife worked early and usually left the house before the kids were up, so it was Carly's younger sister, "Joni," who found her.

I'll never forget that day in the early 2000s, three weeks after Carly's death, when Jamie first walked into my office. I was a bit scared. I didn't know what to say to a grieving parent, a person going through unthinkable pain, so it seemed best to simply go ahead. I had already arranged my treatment room with pillows on the floor. Now I burned sage to clear the space and lit a candle. I drummed and called in the four directions and the center to set up sacred space. As I continued to drum, I entered the trance state that is known to shamanic people around the world as the dreamtime, or non-ordinary reality, or the shamanic state of consciousness. I traveled to the upper world, a dimension in the spirit realm that is above us, and where benign spirits wait to help us. I went to the cave of my teacher in this realm, the goddess Isis, and behold, sitting right beside her was Carly. I described her to Jamie, along with the iridescent, royal-blue dress she was wearing, which he recognized. She said to let her dad know that her death was part of the plan. She was sorry it had caused so much hurt and pain, but she wasn't meant to live a long life this time. As she spoke and I repeated what she said to Jamie, I was aware of his body relaxing. I didn't realize I was crying, but when I came back from the journey I had tears all over my face. I held Jamie and we both cried.

We sat in the dim candlelit office for several hours while Jamie told me about his daughter and that what I said was "right on." Years later, Jamie said that session was like water to someone dying of thirst. He has remained a dear friend ever since.

Even as soon as this session, three weeks after Carly's death, Jamie had already learned that, "There may not be a tomorrow, so if you are interested in something, you just have to 'go for it.'" Jamie has since used the lesson of his daughter's death to live more into the truth of his heart - not that he hasn't had ups and downs. Grief can show up in unexpected ways, and everyone grieves differently. Jamie has spent dark days in bed, wanting to end his own life. Grief can also shine a light on things that are not working, which is what happened with Jamie and his wife, who are now divorced. People often say that the death of a child can break up a marriage, but I am not sure that is true. Rather, I think an emotional crises makes it harder to fool ourselves about the basic structure of our lives. Profound pain brings us to the deepest reality of our being.

Carly's spirit has often shown up in my journeys, even when I am not traveling for Jamie, and I wonder why, as I never met her in this life. She wears a long, royal-blue dress made out of some filmy fabric. I often see her in the temple of Isis, where she always seems busy, carrying things or cleaning something. She has the quality of a dove as she flits about the temple. Whatever she does, she seems to bring order and peace. She seems pleased that Jamie and I have remained friends.

Dove Tail - the journey

This point is in the center of the upper abdomen, about an inch below the sternum. I sink into the point and find myself slipping into cool, silky blue water. The water feels thicker and softer than water usually does, and it is soothing to my skin. I lie back and float for a few minutes, until a large dove comes and lands beside me on the water. I ask if she is the spirit of the point, and she chirps, then indicates that I should crawl onto her back. So I do. As we take flight, I look down at the blue pool of water. The whole landscape glows like a day in early spring. The colors are vibrant, there is a cool breeze, and the sun is shining brightly. We land in the top of a tall tree, where Dove shows me her nest. There are four eggs in it and she settles gently upon them.

Her thoughts come to me by telepathy: I am the mother dove, who patiently warms the eggs until they hatch. What are your eggs? What must you keep warm until it hatches? My long tail feathers fan out in an arc connecting all seasons that are processing in your body and your life, and as I connect them, I bring peace and contentment. I can fly high and give you a lofty perspective. As I am for my babies in this nest, I am also your reliable protector. I will never go far away.

These thoughts streamed into me as I sat peacefully in the tree, absorbing the beauty all around. I felt all stress and anxiety lift. I thought about Carly in the temple and how peaceful she is. She has no stress or anxiety. I thought about Jamie and how hard it must be to lose a child, and how he misses her so much sometimes that he wants to die, while at other times he moves forward playing his music.

Dove's thoughts come again: Carly is like a dove now: She brings peace. This point will bring peace to the suffering, to those who have had heavy blows to the heart. It will comfort and warm their hearts and it will help them warm the eggs of their ideas, until the ideas hatch and joy fills their lives.

Dove brings me back to the blue pool and I return to myself.

This point, Dove Tail, is in a place just below the sternum that is very vulnerable. If someone punches you there in just the right way, the blow can kill. Yet, paradoxically, the point is closely associated with the Official called The Heart Protector, which fields all the insults and injuries life throws at us, so that they will not harm the Heart. Mothers are like that with their children. They won't let *anything* harm the children. If you have ever met a wild animal who is protecting her young, then you know how fierce this energy can be.

How does such ferocity fit into the concept of Yin? It's inherent, because Yin comprises the dark, night, passive energy, and clearly this point is about protection - which if threatened can be very aggressive. There cannot be Yin without Yang, or Yang without Yin. If you look at the symbol for Yin/Yang you'll see a little white dot in the black and a little black dot in the white. So as we think of Dove Tail, most of the time it is a peaceful place, mom sitting gently on the eggs. The scene is soft, warm, and quiet. However, let something threaten the peace, and the bit of Yang within the Yin will rise up and show its teeth.

Chapter 20: Initiation to Spirit - Wind Palace - (Governor Vessel 16)

When I was 5 years old, I lived in Arlington, Texas, where my father was stationed at the Naval Air Base. We had moved there from Massachusetts. It was 1963, and our president was John F. Kennedy.

The day was a normal day for a 5 year-old. I had gotten home from kindergarten. My grandmother, Nana, was puttering in the kitchen, and my mom was working in Dallas. The phone rang and Nana picked it up. Her gasp caught my attention. She was weeping, and I knew something terrible had happened. My mom had called from the city, where President Kennedy had been shot. My mom was there in the crowd. I don't remember when my parents got home; I hardly remember anything else about the day except the gasp and the tears. That is, until that night.

I was sleeping when I suddenly woke up. There was a man standing at the foot of my bed. I started to scream, until he spoke to me. I recognized the accent, being from Massachusetts. The man said he felt my calling. He vanished. Now I did scream!

"You just have an overactive imagination, honey," Mom said. "There are no such things as ghosts, and with all the news about President Kennedy, you were just scared."

"You do realize" - Two Moons, one of my teachers in ordinary reality, said when I told him this story - "that if you had been born in a tribal culture and you experienced this, they would have taken it very seriously. You would have been immediately taken to the village Shaman for training."

"Instead, my mom took me to a psychiatrist when I was 15 years-old, partly by my request - I thought a psychiatrist might know something about 'psychic phenomenon' - and partly because my mom was concerned about me hearing voices."

Two Moons laughed. "What did the psychiatrist say?"

"He told my mom that I had an overactive imagination and that I was reading the wrong books." I laughed too.

"Your spirit chose to be born to a family where you didn't fit. That forced you to look to yourself, to walk alone, to discover the Shaman's cave inside yourself."

"I did for awhile as a teenager. I had one friend who was another misfit. However, my desire to be loved was too addictive and I sold out to fundamental Christianity and a marriage to someone who wasn't right for me."

"What woke you up?"

"Acupuncture. My first treatment, in 1989, cleared the fog. It reminded me who I was, and it started me on this path. In Acupuncture school, a teacher who was a Shaman and an Acupuncturist (Eliot Cowan, author of *Plant Spirit Medicine*) taught our class how to do a shamanic journey. I felt like I had come home."

"You did," he affirmed.

After I graduated from Acupuncture school, I started attending any and all classes I could find on Shamanism. At a reunion of my Acupuncture class, we invited Eliot to teach us again. During that class, he introduced the idea of using shamanic journeying to visit the spirits of Acupuncture points. The point we journeyed to is on the Governor Vessel. It is found in a pit right at the base of the skull, in the very center where the spine joins the head. Like Dove Tail it is a very vulnerable spot, so much that needling it is forbidden. The point's name is Wind Palace.

Wind Palace - the journey

I struggle to reach the next ledge (actually a vertebra) and pull myself up. Some areas of the cliff are smooth, others rough. I am almost there. One last foothold and I stand up at the top and look down into the hollow center. I do not feel ready to enter Wind Palace, though I know I must step off and trust. As I think about it, my animal guide gives me a shove. I fall swirling through the center of a whirlwind and land in the bottom of a round room. The ceiling is very high with stained glass windows close to the top. A figure made of light floats down on the sun beams coming through the windows. I stand and face him as he glides to just in front of me. He takes my hands and we begin to dance - a waltz. We are riding on the air, as light as the wind itself.

"This point is the place for those who are ready for the winds of change to take them higher," he says. "They must be ready to trust. They must not be weighed down too heavily with their burdens or they'll never dance on the wind. If you bring them to my palace too soon, the winds will tear them apart."

We finish dancing and as he bows to me, I curtsy in response. Floating back on the light I find my animal guide waiting. We climb back down the vertebrae in the back of the neck and I return to ordinary reality.

As I think about this journey I am reminded of Cat Steven's song, "I listen to the Wind." Wind in Chinese medicine can be an external cause of illness, but wind is also a necessary force of nature. The winds of change is a phrase I have always loved; I think about it when the weather changes often wind precedes or follows after the change. To stand outside in heavy wind can be a powerful experience. I understand why the spirit says to only offer this point when someone is ready for that power.

Section 7: Autumn - Again

Joni Mitchell's song, "Circle Game" talks about the seasons going around and around each year and there's nothing we can do to stop the movement. We can look back from where we came, as we move through the seasons.

I could make a case for starting in any one of the seasons, as it doesn't really matter because life is a circle. We always come back around to where we started, over and over and over. The number of cycles around the seasons constitutes our age.

So here we are in Autumn again. Once again the leaves are painting a magnificent picture of reds, oranges, and yellows. Once again the air turns crisp and clean. The smell of smoke from fireplaces fills the air in the evenings, and people gather around tables groaning with the bounty that was harvested back in the late summer. Autumn is a time of gratitude -- and not only in America, for while other countries may not have the "Thanksgiving story," every tradition has some way to celebrate the abundance Earth provides to help us survive the coming cold.

As we come around to Autumn each year, we ask: What will I let go of this year? What physical, mental or emotional baggage have I been dragging around that keeps me from living life to its fullest? What will I store to nourish myself in the Winter?

What has value and is precious to me? What losses still bring tears to my eyes and tightness in my chest? How can I honor what was lost, so the pain may ease a bit? What inspires me? What brings a sense of the divine into my life and brings me to the place where there are no words, simply an "ah"?

Ah-tumn. Full circle from the beginning of this book. What will you take with you from these stories? What served you? What didn't resonate? Let it go.

As one travels around the seasons, year after year, when we come to Autumn, we need remember to make an assessment. Let go of what brings no joy and life to us, and remember that we are creating space for something new to arise in the Spring. Keep only what is life giving and will nourish you through the Winter.

I would like to share two more points and stories from the Autumn to help us move full circle. Seasons are not linear - they continue to circle. Be in each season as fully as possible. Don't try to do Summer in Winter, nor to create new things in Autumn instead of Spring. Allow each season to guide us in becoming our highest, fullest, and most alive selves.

Chapter 21: Welcome Fragrance: (Large Intestines 20)

The information gathered by most of our senses travels through an organized system of nerve synapses, and winds up at parts of the brain where our intellect intervenes to tell us what we sensed. So if I look at a dress in a store, the information my eyes gather goes through this process until I can speak or think, "A blue velvet dress, with antique, ivory lace, long sleeves, and a calf length hem." This process does not apply to smells, however. There is no intellectual component to what we smell. Rather, when a smell trips off a neuron, that neuron takes the signal directly to the primitive (reptilian) brain. I have heard that this trait goes back to a time in our evolution when the sense of smell would warn us if something was poisonous, or if another person was a threat - it served our survival, basically. In any case, it is our sense of smell that evokes the most intense emotions and memories - instantly. When I smell cinnamon, I am immediately back in my grandmother's kitchen, and there's a hot apple pie in the oven.

When I was in acupuncture school, our program was set up in three week intensives. We would travel to Miami, stay in vacation rentals, do a semester's worth of work in three weeks flat, and then go back home and do our best to absorb what we'd just crammed in. My daughters were 9 and 4 when I started, so they stayed with my parents when I went to school. I remember the first time I was away, when I got home, my 9 year old came running up and started smelling my arms. When I asked her what she was doing, she said, "Mommy, I missed your smell."

Smells are part of diagnosis in acupuncture too. In school we each brought in small containers of something interesting to smell. There were bags of cut up onions and garlic, there were lemons, there were spices, there were cleaning products, and cookies, old oil and fish oil, vitamin pills, pennies, terrarium water, and on and on. We spent a day smelling each item and putting them into categories according to the five elements (scorched, fragrant, rotten, putrid, and rancid). This day was supposed to help us recognize the elemental smells on one another, on people in general, and eventually our patients. Several of my teachers have said over the years that smell was their weakest sense.

I hear this same statement now as a teacher both from students and colleagues, and I say it is a "story". In other words, people declare that smell is their weak sense and then act on that belief, ignoring smells and thus creating a "disability" -- except that we all smell, all the time. We decide what to pitch from the refrigerator, based on how it smells. We decide whether we can wear an article of clothing one more time, based on how it smells. We can tell if someone owns a cat by how their home smells. We know we have stepped in poop left by an inconsiderate dog owner, by the smell. Often we can tell if our child is ill, by a particular hot, metallic smell. It is a matter of attention, and in the first world, we've been taught not to pay attention to personal odors.

As part of the teaching, most Americans live or work in buildings with filtered air; we plug "deodorizers" into our wall sockets; we put deodorants and perfumes on our bodies; and we live with a myriad of other chemicals designed to cover up what we have been taught are "bad" smells. No wonder many people think they can't smell.

In addition to the masking chemicals, children are often told they are wrong when they use their sense of smell. When I was five or six years old, we lived next door to a woman who thought I was just the *cutest* thing, and she always wanted to hug and kiss me. I resisted, because to me she smelled really bad. I still remember the smell: it was very sweet, even cloying - metabolites of alcohol, I know as an adult, and my parents have since told me she was in fact an alcoholic. Nonetheless, at the time they insisted that I had to let her touch me, so as not to be rude. In effect, they were telling me to ignore my instinctual knowing "of some kind of problem here." It was a different time, and my parents only did what everyone else was doing at the time, nowadays educated parents are less likely to force a child to hug someone just to not be rude.

Think of the phrases we use about smelling: "I smell something fishy," or, "I smell a rat," or, "What a sweet [smelling] deal." These phrases date back to a time when humans used their sense of smell to know when someone was lying, fearful, happy, mournful, etc. This information did, and still can, help us make appropriate decisions.

So, we have not lost our ability to smell, I conclude: we have simply ignored or neglected it. You can awaken it however. Just go outside (or stay inside) and smell everything. I mean *everything*. Notice what your body does when you smell something. Do memories resurface? Does your face crinkle up? Does your throat tighten? Do you want to breathe more deeply? Smelling is one of the most glorious gifts we have. It enhances our entire existence if we let it.

Welcome Fragrance - the journey

When the drumming CD starts, I begin from my nose: the point is on the face, just beside the nostrils on both sides. If you touch the area gently, you'll find it: a soft little indentation that feels like it "wants" your fingertip. I slip into the point and find myself floating on a cloud of scent. (Think of to a cartoon image of someone floating on a waft of baking pie.) Then I land softly in a field of flowers with a fragrance so strong I am almost nauseated.

I stand and look around. The flowers go on and on in every direction, so I pick a direction and start walking. My animal is next to me and he sneezes, once and then again. He walks a little faster, sneezing a third time. When we come to a lake, by unspoken agreement we jump right in -- in my case clothes and all -- to wash off that awful smell. The lake is small, so we swim to the other side, which is flower free, and lie on the bank to dry off. The sun is warm on my skin, though the air has an edge of coolness - it must be Indian Summer. There is a forest behind us, and I notice bright red, yellow, and orange leaves blowing around.

Another smell begins subtly entering my nose and I am suddenly in a bedroom, lying in a canopy bed with lace pillow cases and filmy curtains tied to the bedposts. I feel small, like a child. The bed is spongy and soft and the smell grows stronger: it is like baby powder. I hear a movement to my left and sit up - it's my my Nana, she is applying baby powder to her back and shoulders and underarms.

"Nana, I have missed you so much!" I exclaim.

She turns to look at me and says, "You were only asleep for a few minutes and I didn't go anywhere."

I am confused, until I look down at my hands and see that they are child hands. I remember suddenly the time I spent a weekend with Nana when I was nine years old. I slept with her in her canopy bed, and there was baby powder everywhere. As I cozy back into her pillows, the experience fades and I am back on the bank of the lake.

Standing before me is a smallish woman, similar in build to my Nana, and she even smells of baby powder. She has short grey hair and wire rimmed glasses. Her rosy cheeks are accentuated by her smile. "Are you the spirit of this point?" I ask.

"Yes, darling." Nana used to say that in the very same way. I feel tears.

"Sweetheart," she says, "you can have Nana with you all the time. Every time you smell something that reminds you of her, you can have delicious memories of her. Welcome them."

"Is that what your medicine is about?"

"Smells are a wonderful gift, you know." She goes on, "Your sense of smell can tell you if something is poisonous, or spoiled, or bad for you. It can tell you if you are in danger, or if something is good for you. It can literally take you back through your memories to experience once again the love and joy you once knew. Imagine how dull life would be without this sense. You wouldn't even be able to taste your food."

She starts to walk down a path in the colorful woods - fall colors are blasting everywhere, vibrant with change.

"People walk through life," she continues, "believing that smells should only be sweet, like walking through that field of flowers -- which can be nice for a time, but then it gets overwhelming, so you can't smell anything else. Many of your patients have forgotten how to welcome smells. Just as the colors of these trees wake up your sense of sight, smells wake us up to the immense variety of being alive."

We enter a cave on the side of a hill, bending very low to get in. But once we enter we can stand up straight, and she leads me down a tunnel lit by torches. My animal guide is following; I can hear his soft padding on the rock floor. Soon we reach a great chamber that is sparkling with gemstones. I notice as I look more closely at the cavern that each gemstones can slide out with just a soft tug, so that they are actually small containers. I open one and smell rain in summer as it hits hot cement.

I am instantly in Texas, seven years old and riding my bicycle on the sidewalk. It has just started raining, and I hear my mother calling for me to come in. As I ride up the driveway I smell and see the mimosa tree in the front yard. The mimosa! I'd forgotten I spent hours sitting in that tree when I was this age. The experience fades.

Back in the cavern, I find I have closed the crystal container and replaced it on the wall. The woman says to me, "Every smell known to the world is stored in this cavern. When you use this point for your patients, you open the world to them through their sense of smell. Their life experiences will become richer and more connected to memories, to enhance their lives in the here and now."

I want to stay in the cavern and try all the smells, one after another, but both my animal and the woman urge me to leave. As we exit the cavern and I hear the drumbeats calling me back to my body.

I open my eyes and turn off the CD player.

I will go back to that point again! I want to smell and relive more memories. I have used this point on a patient who thought she lost her sense of smell, it came back! She was so happy.

Chapter 22: The Gifts - Fish Region: (Lung 10)

When I moved out of my parents' house for the first time, at age 18, it was to become a missionary in a "cult" I had joined as a senior in high school. They sent me to Southern California with another woman and two men, the oldest of us being 25. Our little core group was charged with starting a group of worshippers. We were required to get part time jobs to support ourselves, then to spend the majority of our time out "witnessing." Witnessing involved knocking on doors, hanging around in parks, canvasing college campuses, and generally trying to get people to come to our place for a "bible study."

My job was at a fast food joint called "Jack-in-the-Box." Minimum wage was $1.69 an hour, gas was $.55 a gallon, and cigarettes about $.55 a pack - yes I smoked in those days. It was hard to make ends meet, working part-time at minimum wage. Because I didn't have money for food, I ate discarded burgers at work. By law they had to discard food after a certain amount of time, if it hadn't been sold.

When Christmas rolled around, I realized I didn't have enough money to buy gifts for the people I was living with, or for the young man I had met and started dating. So after much thought, I took a little money and went to the art supply store, where I bought what I needed to make my gifts. I don't remember everything I made anymore, but I do remember knitting a macrame' purse for my female roommate. She had given me some lush, golden velvet fabric to recover her chair. The fabric was antique and had belonged to her great aunt, and when the chair was recovered there was some fabric leftover, which I used to line the purse.

My boyfriend let me use his apartment to work in. I would turn on his stereo and sit on the floor tying macrame knots to make this gift. I was excited as I worked, watching the purse evolve into a work of art that I was proud to offer my friend. Once it was finished, I wrapped it in the comic section of my boyfriend's newspaper, as I had no money for wrapping paper.

On Christmas morning, I could hardly breathe with excitement as people opened my hand-made gifts, and I remember thinking that this was one of the best Christmases I had ever had. Now, when I think back on this Christmas, I realize that the reason it was so wonderful was that I put so much of myself into it.

At the time, I thought I was "saving money," but in years to come, I would often give hand-made gifts. Indeed, I still do, for I have seen that gifts made by the giver are precious; they contain the essence, intention, and love of the giver. These gifts are unique, one-of-a-kind, and often have visible flaws. Many times it is those very flaws that make the gift special.

In a world of mass-produced, slave-labor, imported-from-the-East products, it is easy to forget the joy of shaping something with your own hands, pouring your soul into it, and offering it to another.

There is an Amish market near where I live in Annapolis. One section sells meats, produce, and pastries, while the other sells hand-made furniture, home goods, and quilts. The quality of these items far surpasses anything mass-produced. Not only that — they weren't shipped thousands of miles to get here, using precious resources our children will need.

I always think of this point, Fish Region, when I think of these Amish-made goods. The Chinese character we read as "Fish Region" represents a great and priceless fish that is fed only to royalty. It is a one-of-a-kind fish, not one plucked from a net containing hundreds of fish. This fish is specially looked for and can only be found by someone who wants to serve the King. And while this point is a metal point from the season of Autumn, it is also a fire point within the metal. "Fish Region" comes to the patient like a golden vessel containing hot brandy to warm the soul. It is a gift from the heart.

Fish Region - the journey

This point which is on the palmar surface of the hand, nestled into the middle of the pad at the base of the thumb. Drifting on drumbeats I slip into the point. Once in, I find myself standing near the bow of a massive sailing ship. It is a sunny day, and the ship's captain stands nearby, the breeze blowing back his hair as he watches the sea. My animal and I walk up to him and ask if he is the spirit of the point.

He looks at me and says, "No, I am not. The cook is the spirit of the point and I am helping him with his mission. He is down below, so you should go talk with him. I am sailing to the Fish Region, just past Very Great Abyss."

I walk to the hatch and climb down the ladder, to find the cook searching through recipe books.

I announce myself and ask him about his medicine.

"I'm busy," he snaps. "I am in the middle of our annual voyage to retrieve the King of the Halibut. It is reported that this year the King Halibut is 8 feet long and weighs about 400 pounds."

"Why is this annual voyage for a fish so important?" I ask.

He looks at me as though I am the most stupid creature he has ever met. He hurrumphs and feigns patience. "Because the King and Queen always have the king Halibut in the Autumn for their feast of Fish Region."

I am a little bewildered, so I sit down with my power animal and wait for more information, which does not come, and soon the rocking of the ship and the sound of the waves slapping the hull have lulled me to sleep. I am out cold with my head on my power animal by the time someone bellows down the hatch, "Fish Ahoy! He's been spotted!!!"

The cook jumps up and scurries up the ladder, so I groggily follow. I look out to where both captain and cook are looking, and I see the largest possible fish leap out of the water and back. The surprise wakes me up -- this fish actually wears a gold crown! The crown is jewel-encrusted and sparkles in the sunlight, so bright that for a moment I think I must have imagined it. My power animal tells me that no, I really did see it. (I say to myself, Of course, if an animal can talk to me, a fish can wear a crown.)

Now I notice a team of fishermen being lowered in a small boat that will carry them over the waves to the fish. Some will be rowing while others hold. They are eager to catch this prize. The creature leaps again, as if to taunt the seamen, and one of them shoots and misses. I can almost hear laughter from the deep. The captain, the cook, and I are breathlessly watching from the bow.

The King halibut is so sure of himself that he jumps again -- but alas, a spear pierces his flank. He struggles, pulling taut the rope that is attached to the spear. The water is cloudy with blood as the fishermen pull on the line and the oarsmen struggle to keep the boat afloat and steady. The situation is perilous as this massive fish fights with all his might to escape, while his lifeblood keeps spilling and his power weakens. I can feel my adrenalin pumping. My breathing is fast, my heartbeat bangs in my throat, and I taste something bitter. I almost can't look as the men hang onto the spear for dear life as this beast of a fish, it must weigh about the same as three of them, thrashes and tows the little boat around like a toy. The King halibut is pulling them toward the coast, with the obvious intention of bashing the boat against the rocks. Finally one fisherman aims and hits him with a second spear, and this time the wound is lethal. A loud cheer rings out, and I look around to see the entire crew lined up along the side of the ship. A second boat is lowered to take more crew members out to help bring in the noble, lifeless body.

All that afternoon the cook and his men are preparing the fish as we sail back into port, where we find the sun low in the sky and the townspeople gathered at the dock. They are singing songs about fishing expeditions of the past, and many are waving handmade flags and banners with embroidered fish.

The evening meal takes place in a grand banquet hall, with the King and Queen sitting at the head of the table. The fish has been cut up and circulates on several large platters, up and down the table. The platter before the King and Queen holds only the fish's crown. The King holds up the crown and the assembly cheers. I notice similar crowns mounted all around the room, presumably from expeditions past.

I am not sitting at the table. I am standing aside watching the event, and at that moment an arm comes around my shoulders. I look to see the Cook beside me, this time smiling and relaxed. He says, "This point means -- nothing but the best, no matter how difficult or how long it takes'.

"Your patients will know they deserve the best when you offer this point." He walks away and stands by the table. The King rises and asks the people to honor the cook. All applaud, and he makes a ceremonial bow to the King.

My power animal and I leave and I return to myself.

Dear ones, don't ever forget: You deserve the best. We all do, and this journey reminds me of the fun and adventure of finding and serving each other and ourselves the best in life.

Chapter 23: Wrapping it up

All these points live in us. When I am treating a patient, I don't create *Fish Region,* or *Dove Tail* in the moment, I am only touching something that is already there. In the acupuncture school we often tell the patients the students treat, that they did a great job. They usually say, "I didn't do anything but just lie here." We all smile knowingly, yes they did do something. All the needle does is awaken the point which is already there. Yes, the practitioner has to know from observing the patient, listening to them, feeling their pulses, etc., which point or points might be the best to awaken in that moment. Once awake though, all the work is done within the patient by their own body, mind, and spirit.

I was supervising a student one time whose patient had an energy block, between the Conception Vessel and the Governor Vessel. The reader will remember, I said when those two are blocked, treatment on any of the other meridians will do nothing. The student was afraid of doing this block, because of the location of the points. I told her she had to do the points to break the block next week, when the patient was supposed to come back. So, over the course of the week, she went around talking to everyone who had either had that treatment, or who had done that treatment, to glean from their experiences. She envisioned herself doing the treatment, many times on this patient. The following week when the patient came in, the block was gone! That block had been present for more than a month and the student was avoiding treating it, these blocks don't just disappear on their own. This student had treated the patient entirely with intention!

I tell you that story because, you the reader, have just had all the points you just read about, treated, by the intention of reading them. So if one chapter resonated more than another, that might be one for you, to read again.

In Quantum Physics, we know that the observed is affected by the observer. In acupuncture, the points are directed, by the intentions of the practitioner. And, the intention of the patient is to feel better, so this also affects the treatment. Although the patient doesn't have to "believe" in acupuncture for it to work. Animals are treated with acupuncture and respond beautifully, and they don't know one way or the other about "believing".

There are many mysteries in this world which are difficult to explain, but we know from experiences and observation, over and over, there is *something* going on. There will always be people, who want concrete answers, they will go on to run experiments, find answers, which then, of course, leads to more questions. Bless them. If it weren't for people like them, we might still be beheading people, for saying the Earth is round.

I am not one of those who has to have all the answers. I know, what I need to know, will be there when I need to know it. For me acupuncture and the use of these points is like having a rich pallet, with many colors of paint, and the way I mix it, creates beautiful pictures. I am hoping that this book has given you a glimpse of that beauty, and a realization that, that beauty already lives and flourishes, inside of you.

About The Author

Deanna Stennett was born in the Boston area in 1958. The oldest of three children, she learned leadership qualities from being in charge of her siblings, when her mother went back to work. She was the child of a military father during the Vietnam conflict and so she lived in Massachusetts, Texas, Florida, Maryland, and California.

At 18, Deanna joined a "cult" group and was sent to Los Angeles, CA. She stayed there after leaving the group at age 21. Here she met her first husband and had her two daughters. Before getting married, Deanna was studying Art with the intention of being an Art teacher. When the marriage dissolved, Deanna and her daughters moved back to the East coast to live with her parents (where they retired) in Middleburg, Florida (outside of Jacksonville). Having been a stay at home mother for 8 years, Deanna intended to go to the University of North Florida to finish her Art degree and become an Art Therapist. Her new acupuncturist suggested Acupuncture school. At the thought of this, she felt her heart do a "happy dance". She knew she found the path that was hers.

It was in Acupuncture school that she learned about shamanism, and she has been practicing both modalities since 1993. In

1995, she bought an acupuncture practice in Anne Arundel county, Maryland and moved there with her second husband and daughters. She began teaching at Maryland University of Integrative Health (formerly Tai Sophia Institute) in the acupuncture program in 1999.

Deanna's second marriage also dissolved and she moved to Annapolis, where she currently resides. In 2010, Deanna earned her Master's Degree in Transformative Leadership and Social Change, which is where she began this book as her Thesis Project.

Deanna lives near Sandy Point State Park with her current partner, her stepson, her dog and three cats. They have a vegetable garden, and bees. The next step will be chickens.

Deanna still teaches at Maryland University of Integrative Health, and runs a busy acupuncture practice in Annapolis. She teaches workshops and classes in shamanism, including an in-depth 2 year program, and also offers shamanic healing sessions.

Endorsements from other Authors for the outside back cover:

«Deanna Stennett gifts us with this beautifully written book *Poetry of the Body*. Through story telling and sharing metaphors Deanna teaches us about the connection and relationship between acupuncture points and how they are connected to the cycles of life and nature. She inspires us to explore the relationship with the magic in our body deepening our connection with our self and our place in the world. Brilliant book!"

Sandra Ingerman, MA, author of *Soul Retrieval* and *Walking in Light*

"People who think acupuncture is just about needles and points on the body will gain a whole new perspective when they encounter the stories and personal experiences that Deanna Stennett offers in this ground-breaking book. With a deep, rich background in shamanic practices, she opens new doors into this timeless and ancient healing modality."

Tom Cowan, author of *Shamanism as a Spiritual Practice for Daily Life* and *Yearning for the Wind: Celtic Reflections on Nature and the Soul*.

"Energy and Spirit flow through everything and carry the profound wisdom needed to bring mind, body, emotions, and soul into balance. *Poetry of the Body* is an inspiring search and discovery story of that balance. Written in a down-to-earth, personal style with deep compassion for the human experience and mystery of life, this book is a potent source of wisdom for us all."

Colleen Deatsman, author of *The Hollow Bone: A Field Guide to Shamanism* and *Seeing in the Dark: Claim Your Own Shamanic Power Now and in the Coming Age.*